FIFTIES *Fins*

DENNIS DAVID

MBI Publishing Company

First published in 2001 by MBI Publishing Company, Galtier PLaza, Suite 200, 380 Jackson Street, St. Paul, MN 55101-3885 USA

MBI Publishing Company books are also available at discounts in bulk quantity for industrial or sales-promotional use. For details write to Special Sales Manager at Motorbooks International Wholesalers & Distributors, Galtier Plaza, Suite 200, 380 Jackson Street, St. Paul, MN 55101-3885 USA.

Library of Congress Cataloging-in-Publication Data Available

ISBN 0-7603-0961-2

Edited by Amy Glaser
Designed by Bruce Leckie

Printed in China

On the Front Cover
Cadillac's sculptured fin design was the work of GM designer Dave Holls. Holls began work with GM under the guidance of the legendary Harley Earl and would help see the fin through to its very end in 1964. The twin taillight design accented by loads of chrome and stainless steel had no equal in the fin wars. Cadillac's fin would see a gradual decline after 1959.

On the Frontispiece
DeSoto's rear quarter was a perfect blend of trim work that in later years would prove to be a hit at any car show. A triple taillight theme set off by angular lines and gold anodized trim set the top-of-the-line Adventurer convertible apart from the competition. Despite its wonderful style and solid reputation, DeSoto was only a few short years away from its ultimate demise.

On the Title Page
Not to be lost in the fin wars, Plymouth's Belvedere line carried a stylish fin that was a dramatic sweep beginning at the front end. Proving to be one of the most popular cars of the day, Plymouth would build 443,799 cars in 1958. Powerful engines were once again the order of the day, as the Belvedere was powered by a 317.6-cubic-inch V-8 that generated 225 horsepower. In later years, a movie based on the novel by Stephen King entitled Christine *would scare theatergoers everywhere with a haunted 1958 Plymouth Fury.*

On the Contents Page
The first fin to ever appear on a car was on a1948 Cadillac.

On the Back Cover
Oldsmobile's top-of-the-line offering for 1956 was the Series 98 Starfire convertible. At $3,380, it was expensive, but came with Oldsmobile's 324-cubic-inch Rocket V-8 that was rated at 240 horsepower. The Rocket engine was used for many racing endeavors, and famed driver Lee Petty would set a new record at Daytona in the flying mile at 144 miles per hour driving an Oldsmobile. The use of two-tone paint schemes and a unique taillight treatment made for an attractive package. Oldsmobile made only 8,581 Starfire convertibles for 1956, and this example is finished in Black and Alcan White.

CONTENTS

ACKNOWLEDGMENTS

Books like this are not written without the help of many others. Indeed it is through their assistance that I have been able to provide the reader with this in-depth look at Detroit's marvelous fins. I wish to thank my good friends and colleagues Kit Foster and Mike Lamm for their help and encouragement. They are two of the great automotive journalists of all time. My good friends Dr. Paul Sable, Mark Patrick, Jonathan Stein, and Don Keefe also contributed greatly to the endeavor. Thanks also to Bruce and Genia Wennerstrom, co-chairs of the Greenwich Concours de Elegance. Special thanks also to my editor, Keith Mathiowetz. The idea for *Fins* was his, but the pleasure was mine.

Special thanks to all of the car owners who willingly gave their time at all hours of the day in order to get that one special shot: Ralph Bortugno; Charles and Jo-Ann Kraynack; Bob Heuer; Rocco Mancini; John R. Cote; Douglas Marr; Jack and Barbara Lane; Wade Jacobs; Joe and Patrick Conetta; Karen Hubbell; Philip Ciaffaglione; Art Brucato Jr.; Noel and Starr Evans; Bob and Linda LaMadeleine; Jack and Pat David; Don and Ruth Jack; James and Arlene Hamelin; John and Pat Kelley; James Ricci; Paul and Linda Accarpio; Phil Lefebvre; Ralph Perillo; Don and Diane Bouchard; Albert Dellabianca; Donna Hohider; Charles Andrews; Bob and Priscilla Pepler; Ray Mitchell; Mike Davis; Tom Lorgrippo; Eric Stoldt; Neil Carrano; Todd Depino; Leo Boudreau; Bob Majeski; Tony Vespoli; Bud and Stasia Motuzick; Rick Cyr; Bernie Roselli; and Richard Hall.

Special thanks also to my good friend Nicholas E. Pagani, who owns several of the cars featured in this book. When not leasing a portion of his collection out to Hollywood movie projects, he found the time to make his cars available to me.

While this book is filled with the glamorous convertibles and hardtops that seem to define a beautiful car, it also features many sedans and station wagons. Too many books are written only to define a certain segment of the market, but I thought it was important to show that the fin was an intricate part of the automobile in any form.

I'd also like to offer special thanks to my proofreader, who also happens to be my beloved wife, Susan. It is said that everyone in this world has a soul mate. If this is true, then I have certainly found mine. Together we share many hopes and dreams of which this book is just one. I should also thank my special "Hershey Buddy," Chris, my son. Together we have walked countless miles at car shows all over the country. He shares my enthusiasm for the automobile and together we make a team. I wish to dedicate this book to my father, who has always been there for me with words of wisdom and encouragement.

INTRODUCTION

It's hard to pinpoint exactly when it started. Some say it was the slip of a pen that resulted in a slight rise in the rear quarter panel of a Buick or a Cadillac. After all, the stale look of the immediate postwar American automobile was literally crying out for something new. After several years spent building war machines instead of automobiles, Detroit could do nothing more than dust off the old dies and start punching out cars in order to fill the nation's thirst for new automobiles. When that thirst was quenched, the motoring public began demanding more from Detroit. No longer would a car sell on the merits of its dependability alone. It had to have something new, it had to look different, and most of all, it had to represent the direction that America was taking at the time. Airplanes were entering the jet age, washing machines were automatic, and televisions were sitting in most every living room in America. Indeed, America was on a new path, a path that led to a new and brighter future. Aerodynamics would play an important role in taking America to that new future, and the automobile would come to resemble the jet as well.

America was obsessed with the need to go fast. As the age of the jet began to unfold during the 1950s, the quest for speed took on unheard-of proportions. The crossover from piston power to jet propulsion redefined the science of aerodynamics. A close examination of the tail section of

Pontiac used a sculpted masterpiece on the 1957 Bonneville. Heavy use of chrome and a sweeping fin spoke of America's passion for the jet age.

Lockheed's P-38 Lightning shows the beginning indications of a wind-cheating fin, while a modern F-16 is the culmination of that slippery design. Perhaps it was inevitable that automobile design would mimic the aircraft designs of the day. There

In stark contrast to the fin design of 1948, Cadillac's fin for 1960 was a sleek and slender design that was an aerodynamic masterpiece. Through the years the fin saw several different modifications with extensive use of chrome and many variations of taillight themes that stretched the imagination. Again, the fin was taking its cue from the aviation industry as man's quest to go higher and faster resulted in new dimensions in aircraft design.

This is the fin that started it all. Harley Earl's design of the 1948 Cadillac set in motion a styling theme that would last for the next decade. The inspiration for the new design came from Lockheed's P-38 Lightning, which used a number of Cadillac components in its Allison V-1710 engine. Automobile design would continue to be influenced by aviation as the decade of the 1950s witnessed the dawning of the jet age.

By 1963, the fin was finally winding down as evidenced by Studebaker's 1963 Grand Turismo Hawk. The Hawk's fin was a tasteful addition to its overall well-balanced design. While interest in the fin began to wane, the horsepower wars were beginning to evolve as Studebaker offered an R-2 engine package featuring a supercharger. Horsepower was rated at 289 and the Hawk became a serious competitor on the streets.

can be no doubt that the advent of the fin in American automobile styling caused a sensation that has yet to be equaled. Simply put, when we think of the 1950s, we think of fins. While the swept-back wing of the F-86 Sabre may have helped make optimum use of its jet engine, it is highly doubtful that any fin could help a 1959 Cadillac go any faster than its V-8 engine could propel it. No, it wasn't a matter of necessity; it was simply an exercise in the excess of design. However, before the

decade of the 1950s was over, the automobile builders in Detroit would be grafting fins onto cars that would put a fighter jet to shame. While it may have been an excessive use of sheet metal, the automobiles of the 1950s that live in the hearts and minds of people are some of the most sought after collector cars today.

Perhaps it was no accident that the design team at Cadillac constructed a small but noticeable fin on the rear quarter of the 1948 Cadillac. After all, the North American F-86 Sabre had just taken to the skies on October 1, 1947. With its sleek

Chevrolet introduced an all-new body for 1955. The new lineup carried a rather conservative fin that would give way to a sharper jetlike appearance by 1957. Chevrolet offered a number of variations based on its new design including a sedan, hardtop, convertible, and a two-door wagon that was known as the Nomad. All carried the unique tailfin treatment that would propel Chevrolet through the decade of the 1950s and beyond.

well into the early 1950s, when it slowly began to grow into an intricate part of the body. The design work from the Art & Colour Section at General Motors headed by Harley Earl signaled to the rest of Detroit that a change was in the air.

It wouldn't take long for others to catch on, and soon the rest of Detroit would be sprouting fins of their own. Although GM would lead the way for several years, the mid-1950s would see challenges from all of the other manufacturers. Not to be outdone, the Chrysler division mirrored GM's development beginning with the 1955 line-up. Although its bolted-on fin looked more like a home for its taillight than a true fin, it did add to the rear fender's height and length. The Mopar folks knew they were onto something good, and the fin became a major design feature for 1956. By 1957, Chrysler left no doubt that they were a main contender in the fin wars. The battle lines were drawn, and others would also join in the frenzy. By the time it was over, the 1960 Plymouth Belvedere and Fury would have fins that could only be called vertical stabilizers. Tasteful? Maybe not, but they never fail to turn heads at the local car show.

Not one to be left out, Ford saw a vision of its future with the 1949 lineup. A slight lateral bulge in the upper rear fender seemed to grow a little each year. By 1952, the taillight was conspiciously housed in its own jetlike pod that protruded slightly from the rear. For 1955, the beautiful Crown Victoria featured a bladelike fin that ran its entire rear quarter. The stylish Thunderbird also made its debut in 1955, but in a move that could only have been planned obsolescence, its rear fender treatment was somewhat docile. The Thunderbird's fin would grow throughout the 1950s, but so would the car itself. By 1957, the Fairlane would hold a long fin that started with a sweeping curve at the midbody. Ford would use this design feature very

fuselage and swept-back wings, the F-86 gave a strong indication of the future of aviation, but less apparent was the impact that Cadillac's design would have on the automobile. What started as a simple concession to the world of aerodynamics would ultimately end in some of the wildest car designs ever to roll out of Detroit. The little bump on the rear fenders of the late 1940s Cadillacs would remain dormant and almost unnoticeable

Buick created the beautiful Skylark for 1953. It was pure luxury through and through. While Buick would create some of the most radical fins ever during the late 1950s, the tasteful 1953 Skylark used a thicker fin that housed its taillights in two separate pods. Note that the fin's width is still rather wide. In the following years, height would increase while width would decrease, creating a sharper fin.

Motors, a new design for 1958 revealed the unmistakable fin that ran its rear length. A slight change for 1959 revealed a sleeker fin, but a true fin nonetheless. By 1961, the fin was a mere shadow of its former self with only a slight outcropping protruding from the car's rear quarter panel, and in 1962, it was gone altogether.

While Studebaker's merger with Packard in 1954 was something that most Packard purists would choose to forget, it did give both companies a few more years of life in a crowded market. Strangely enough, Studebaker chose to mimic the lower portion of the new jets rather than the upper. A close look at a 1948 Studebaker reveals a taillight that looks more like an exhaust port of a jet rather than a simple taillight assembly. Studebaker would remain docile with its rear fender treatment for a number of years, but would ultimately explode with the 1956 Champion. There was no doubt about it, Studebaker was in the game, and although they wouldn't play for very long, they would produce some stylish cars.

The 1950s would produce the wonderful fin. It was a phenomenon that would know no boundaries. Not only would the leaders use the fin, but also the struggling independents. All of the various divisions would additionally fall into line as Pontiac, Mercury, and DeSoto also sported lateral stabilizers at some point. That the automotive world was left with such a wonderful array of automobiles from this era is truly to the benefit of all. To many it was a time of growth, to others it was a time of innocence, but to car enthusiasts everywhere it was a fascinating exploration of style. The automobile of the 1950s made a statement, and that statement was that length was good, height was better, and loud was OK. Join us as we take a look at the fin and trace its evolution from a humble little sprout to an aerodynamic piece of history.

tastefully during the 1950s, and, like Chrysler, its fin wouldn't reach aircraft proportions until the size of the automobile demanded more of the fin.

Many independent car manufacturers continued to thrive in the early 1950s, but as the struggle to survive became harder for the little guys, the design concession of the fin would cause many to scramble for the funds involved in new tooling. As Nash merged with Hudson to create American

Beginnings of the Fin

1

Many historians have long believed that the tooling of America's war machines for World War II was perhaps the greatest industrial effort in history. Factories that once manufactured everything from children's toys to automobiles were turned into munitions suppliers overnight. In order to assist in the war effort, great automobile companies such as General Motors, Ford, Nash, Packard, and Chrysler would build everything from tanks to bombers. While the war machine raged, Americans kept themselves on wheels by keeping their old

Packard introduced its Twenty-Sixth Series on November 21, 1952. Styling was crisp and clean while the chrome accent strips on the rear quarters gave an indication of the future. By 1958, Packard's last year of production, the fin had grown into a taller vertical sweep that was an intricate part of the body. The demise of Packard was seen as a great loss to the American automobile community. Automobile Quarterly

The new 1948 Series 62 Cadillac was even better with the top down, ready for a drive in the country. After several years of manufacturing battle tanks for World War II, Cadillac unveiled its first new postwar offering on the Series 61, 62, and Fleetwood Sixty Special. Cadillac engine components powered Lockheed's P-38 Lightning, one of America's premier fighter planes for the war. Cadillac also built the M-5 light tank, and later the heavier and more powerful M-24 for the U.S. Army during World War II.

machines running. This involved some serious innovation on the part of many car owners as the struggle to get around became harder and harder during the war years. Used parts were sold at a premium and used car prices rocketed skyward, forcing many to find transportation in the ordinary bicycle.

When the war ended in the summer of 1945, automobile builders faced a car market consisting of many elements that were previously unseen in the automotive industry. An unquenchable thirst for new cars coupled with a mass return of the nation's GIs created a demand for new cars that would take several years to fill.

Add to this the fact that many returning soldiers had pockets full of cash just itching to be spent, and one can begin to see the foundation for a new breed of cars. All of these elements meant that America was ready for a new day. After many years of conservation because of the war effort, America was eager for a little luxury. No longer would gas be rationed, and a new set of tires was only a few dollars away. Homes became more spacious and television sets were in most American households. Yes, the war was over and it was time to celebrate.

When the new-model Cadillac hit the streets in 1948, there was one very noticeable styling characteristic that set it apart from all of the rest. Its long and smooth body was accented by two small humps on top of the rear quarter panels. Conservative Cadillac dealers were aghast when they saw them, but the negative opinions were quickly put to rest when the general public greeted

Kaiser was one of the first to offer a completely new postwar style. While the 1947 introductory model would carry the traditionally rounded prewar lines, improvements would come with the 1951 model. The addition of a chrome spear on the upper rear quarter gave the impression of a small fin. Sadly, Kaiser would not live to see the end of the fin wars as the company would cease production in the United States in 1955. This Kaiser Carolina is one of only 308 built in 1953.

15

them favorably. How did they get there? The answer to that has several versions.

The practical use of the fin had been around for some time prior to its commercialization by Cadillac in 1948. Many land-speed-record cars had made use of the fin in their attempts to stabilize the automobile at high speeds. Giovanni Savonucci, an Italian designer, had also made fins a prominent feature on his Italian Cisitalia in 1947. The fin's influence in American automobile design can be traced to Cadillac, although exactly who was responsible for it is a matter of which version the reader subscribes to.

One version is that during a 113-day strike at GM, Cadillac designer Frank Hershey invited the Cadillac design group out to his farm just north of Detriot to continue working on a new concept for the 1948 Cadillac. During this time Harley Earl often drove out in his own automobile, the Y-Job, to check out the progress on the concept. When

In keeping with America's love affair with high-powered aircraft, Kaiser chose a jet-inspired hood ornament that gave no indication of the lack of power beneath the hood. Power for the Kaiser Carolina came from a 226.2-cubic-inch inline-six rated at 118 horsepower. The Carolina was the bottom of the line for Kaiser while the top was the Dragon. In stark contrast to the Carolina, the Dragon was a lavishly appointed automobile that even featured gold-plated trim.

Ford's tasteful use of the fin for 1953 looked right at home on the elegant Country Squire. The simple design made only a mention of things to come. Ford's fin would grow a little each year until it occupied a substantial portion of the rear quarter panel. This particular wagon has been treated to a full restoration and now plies the country roads with ease.

the strike ended, Hershey went back to the studio and grafted the developing fins onto the full-size clay model of the 1948 Cadillac. Cadillac General Manager Nick Dreystadt and even Harley Earl didn't care for the fin at first, but GM President Charles E. Wilson thought that the fins gave Cadillac a good identity and helped to separate the marque from the other GM divisions.

Another version of the fin's origin, and perhaps the most accurate one, is that GM stylists Frank Hershey and Ned Nickles were working on the

concept at Hershey's special projects studio. Hershey had a tailfin on his concept design for GM's British Vauxhall in 1944. Yet another version tells of Bill Mitchell, Cadillac design stylist, returning from the military in 1945 and introducing a tailfin design for the new Cadillac. Perhaps the most exciting version of the fin is the legend of Harley Earl's design team and the P-38 Lightning.

Prior to World War II, Earl sent a group of stylists from his Art & Colour Section out to Selfridge Field near Detroit to take a look at the new

Elegant use of a woodgrain appliqué added a significant touch of class to the Country Squire. As the decade wore on, the fin would find its way onto everything from convertibles to station wagons.

top-secret Lockheed P-38 Lightning. The P-38 was an unconventional airplane to say the least. Its twin Allison V-1710 engines cranked out 1,475 horsepower, but its real innovations were found in its twin fuselage design. Two long, slender tail booms complete with side-mounted air scoops were capped off at the ends by two rounded vertical stabilizers. The design was sleek and Earl's crew came away favorably impressed with the fluid lines of America's new fighter plane.

Once back in the studio, the artists began a series of sketches that would foretell the cars of the future. The wild lines of the P-38 were drawn in all sorts of dream-style creations. From the stylists' point of view, cars were easy to build on paper. Several drawings were looked upon favorably by Earl, and the P-38–inspired design features were then taken to the next step. A series of 3/8-scale models, known as the "Interceptor" series, were

created from the drawings. Work would have continued uninterrupted except for the Japanese attack on Pearl Harbor on December 7, 1941, which completely altered the course of any new car development. All of Detroit would spend the next several years in service of the government. While this would detract from the progression of the automobile's design, its impact on the automobile's future would become evident in the postwar era.

Cadillac, like all other car builders, spent the war years focusing on war materials. The Cadillac V-8 engine was the weapon of choice for the company's new M-5 tank, which was built for the U.S. Army. Cadillac's most important contribution to the war effort was hardly its well-engineered war products, but rather the astounding speed with which it was able to convert to war production. It took only 55 days for the first M-5 tank to roll off the assembly line at its Clark Avenue assembly plant. It was the first of many tanks, and while it is doubtful that the tanks influenced the design of the tailfin, Cadillac's contribution to the war effort advanced its standing with the American public to a new level. The people who built Cadillac's tanks took great pride in their work, and the men who fought in them had no trouble remembering that their lives had been saved by those incredible tanks when they returned home from the war. Perhaps it was no coincidence that Cadillac built many of the components for the Allison aircraft engine that powered the P-38. The plane that had inspired the fins on the 1948 Cadillac was actually powered by components from Cadillac. When Harley Earl's team took the P-38 tailfin treatment and grafted it onto the 1948 Cadillac, the circle was complete.

Less than two months after Cadillac ended production of the M-42 tank, a brand-new Series 62 four-door sedan was driven off the assembly line on October 17, 1945. It was little more than a

Power for the Country Squire came from Ford's flathead V-8. Horsepower was rated at 110 and the flathead had proven itself a fearsome competitor on the street and on the track. Many racing enthusiasts were partial to the flathead due to its reliability and performance. This flathead V-8 pulls the Country Squire with ease.

warmed-over 1942 model, but it was Cadillac's first new car in three years. Cadillac would build only 1,142 cars in 1945 against standing orders for more than 100,000 cars. The intense effort required to fill orders left little time for the development of a new model and it would be 1948 before Cadillac would offer a new look.

With the war finally over, the race was on to supply the nation with new cars. The only real new car was from Kaiser-Frazer, which offered the nation a new and dramatic automobile. Kaiser-Frazer would experience some degree of success in its beginning years, but would ultimately fall as

the competition caught up. Cadillac would merely pick up where it had left off, and after two years a new design was ready. It made its debut on the Series 61, 62, and Fleetwood Sixty Special. The public did not know the new style as "tailfins" just yet, but the new Cadillacs were a big hit. Conservative Cadillac advertising called the new sensation "rudder type styling." Although it is highly doubtful that any rudder could help the 4,000-pound Cadillacs steer any better, it did help the new style look longer and lower. Harley Earl had a never-ending quest to lower the automobile's profile so that its sleek and sexy lines would display

Even though the independents tried to compete, in the end it proved to be too much. Nash touted its Airflyte design as an alternative to the growing popularity of the fin, but as history shows, the fin would win in the long run. Although stylish in its own way, the 1951 Nash Rambler was still trying to shake the rounded lines of the immediate postwar era. It would take some years, but Nash would eventually develop its own version of the 1950s icon known as the fin.

better. Simply put, Earl thought that the automobile looked best when hugging the ground. These were attributes that he exploited quite successfully on his own personal cars, known as the Buick Y-Job and the LeSabre.

Cadillac's new styling sensation took the nation by storm simply because no one else had it. Those two little rudders planted the seed of a new generation of automobiles. All other postwar designs were caught off-guard. While Cadillac was pursuing its rudder-type styling theme, the independents looked on with worry. Packard continued its prewar design when the 21st series cars were introduced to a favorably impressed public.

Packard would introduce a raised rear quarter panel on its 1951 models, thus entering the fin wars. The style of the day for the independents would become known as the "bathtub" look, due to their obvious similarities to an overturned bathtub. Hudson, Nash, and Studebaker did not possess the working capital for extensive retooling, but were forced to do just that in order to keep up. Taking the bathtub look to the extreme, Nash revealed its all-new postwar design in 1949 with the Airflyte series. Streamlining was the key to the new Nash body style, although in the opinion of many, it occurred at the expense of genuine good looks.

Defining the ultimate in Buick luxury, the 1953 Roadmaster Skylark sport convertible commemorated Buick's 50th anniversary. The Skylark was built on the Roadmaster chassis, but used its own fenders with open wheelhouses that were painted in red or white. Its fin treatment was a tasteful exercise in design, as it had not yet reached gargantuan proportions. All of that would change when the 1958 models were introduced to a public that accepted nothing less than a tailfin that literally looked like a jet.

Of the Big Three, Ford was perhaps the most tasteful in its use of the tailfin. The tradition-minded folks at Ford chose a more conservative approach and their fin designs never reached a proportion that exceeded the car's lines. Ford can be credited with grafting fins onto the rear quarters in a way that was always a pleasant addition to the car. For 1946, Ford used its warmed-over prewar design with some freshening of the front grille work. It would be 1949 before Ford would show some hint of the things to

The direction of the American automobile was clearly evident in many aspects of the Skylark's design. A rocket-inspired theme graced the hood with extensive use of chrome. In a few short years the nation would head for the stars with the flight of a Jupiter rocket in December 1958. Just as the tailfin would grow to unheard-of proportions, hood ornaments would mimic the jet age and space travel as well. The Skylark's hood ornament is no exception.

In typical 1950s fashion, the interior of the 1953 Skylark was a rich assortment of leather and chrome. Buick spared no expense in building the Skylark, which sold new for $5,000. Only 1,690 Skylarks were built for 1953.

come. While Cadillac's "rudder type styling" took a vertical theme, Ford chose a slight bump on the horizontal plane for its new look. While it was little more than a leadoff point for the taillights, Ford did expand on its use. By 1951, it had become a long molding that now was taking up quite a bit of space on the rear quarter panel. When Ford redesigned its lineup in 1952, its rear quarter treatment had a definite vertical styling theme that ended in a round taillight set in a pod that was an integral part of its flowing lines. Ford remained somewhat docile with its fin treatment until 1955 when the rounded lines would give way to more linear vertical design.

Chrysler would end up being the latecomer to the dance. As late as 1952, Chrysler's designs were still void of any hint of the fin. Chrysler would bow in 1953 with a more linear design that gave a small indication of fin design. Virgil Exner was never a man to design in excess, and perhaps he was just testing the waters by adding the chrome fin to the rear quarter of the 1955 lineup. Although Chrysler was late to begin its fin treatment, its 1957 lineup would prove to be a sleek design that would set the pace for many to follow. While it took Chrysler some time to catch up with their body design, they were leading the way in the

The New Yorker featured eight chrome teeth just above the horizontal molding on the rear quarter, which would go on to become a hallmark on the New Yorker for years to come. Chrysler manufactured only 921 New Yorker convertibles for 1956. It was a beautiful car that was favored among those with a few extra dollars to spend. The New Yorker convertible sold new for $4,136.

The heart of the New Yorker was Chrysler's famous Hemi V-8. Cubic inch displacement was increased to 354 in 1956. Horsepower also increased to 280 for the New Yorker, but paled in comparison to the 300B, which cranked out 340 horsepower. Chrysler Hemis would go on to rule the streets during the musclecar era. Although the New Yorker was a powerful automobile, it represented Chrysler luxury at its best.

horsepower race. The letter-series Chryslers were some of the most powerful cars of their day.

World War II had a definite impact on the design of the American automobile, and many of those innovations can be directly traced to the building of faster and better airplanes. Among them was the North American F-86 Sabre, the first jet to enter service for the U.S. Air Force. While the P-38 gave rise to the general fin idea, the F-86 took it to new heights. The F-86 featured lines that were unheard of

in the piston aircraft era. All of its surfaces were swept back to a slippery 35 degrees. Despite being somewhat underpowered, the Sabre's design enabled it to surpass the piston aircrafts' speed with ease. No doubt this fact was not lost on Detroit's car builders, and even if the Sabre's speed wasn't blinding, it looked fast even when it was parked on the tarmac. Just as the Sabre took aircraft design to a new level, the tailfin would do the same for the American automobile. After building faster and better jets, America

Chevrolet introduced a new body for 1955. Riding on a 115-inch wheelbase, the new look was greeted favorably by the general public. The top-of-the-line Bel Air Series featured richly upholstered interiors, chrome spears both fore and aft, and full wheel covers. Power came from Chevrolet's 265-cubic-inch V-8 rated at 162 horsepower. With the 1955 lineup, Chevrolet literally crossed the line into the sleeker and sexier 1950s. Gone were the rounded lines of the immediate postwar era and in came the new linear look that would go on to define the decade.

would become obsessed with space travel, adding yet another chapter to the era of fins.

It would take some time for the idea to catch on, but when it did Detroit simply went wild with the fin. No other styling characteristic would play such a remarkable role in automotive design. Detroit built it, and America loved it. By the mid-1950s, it was clearly evident that something was in the air. As we shall see in the next chapter the fin was taking root, and as America entered the decade of innocence the fin would become a more important aspect to the automobile's design than the engine that made it go. Americans couldn't get enough of that so-called "vertical stabilizer."

In the beginning, it all came back to Cadillac's rudder-type styling. Many automotive historians have often said that Harley Earl's talent was not in the design itself, but was often in the ability to pick the design that the general public would like. To this end, Earl was a master at gauging public opinion. His selection of the two little rudders for the 1948 Cadillac set in motion a styling theme that would take command of the decade to follow. The rudders would grow a little each year until an all-out battle broke out between the car builders for the biggest fin of all. Before it was over, America would be left with some of the finest cars that ever graced the streets.

Chevrolet's fins looked at home with the top up or down on the 1955 Bel Air convertible. The new style proved to be a winner as many motorists bought new Chevys in 1955. Chevrolet would update this design for a few more years until a major restyling in 1958 would add length and weight to the Chevy lineup.

2

The Idea Catches On

As the American public began to notice the ever-increasing length of the automobile during the early 1950s, the fin began to show signs that it was here to stay, at least for a while. Some were starting to demonstrate the growth that would define the fin movement, but most were still built to house the aviation-inspired taillights that were quickly gaining acceptance. What had started as a simple design concession to the aviation

Although the Corvette began its life with a fin-styled taillight pod, styling for 1956 saw the tailfin completely eliminated. The 1954 on the left featured the classic introductory Corvette design, while the 1958 model on the right clearly indicates the Corvette's future. In response to Ford's new Thunderbird, the Corvette received V-8 power in 1955, but it still wasn't enough as the T-Bird's production of 16,155 cars eclipsed the Corvette's production figure of 700.

Cadillac's restyle for 1950 still featured the small P-38–inspired tailfins that defined the infancy of the fin movement. Overall, automobile design was becoming longer and lower, and by the mid-1950s it would change completely as the modern postwar look took over. Cadillac would sell over 100,000 cars for 1950, which clearly demonstrated the fin's growing popularity.

Ford introduced the Thunderbird in 1955 to a motoring public that was swept away by the cute little two-seater. In a shot aimed directly at the Corvette, Ford would sell 16,155 Thunderbirds in the car's introductory year. The tasteful use of chrome and a tiny, but noticeable fin were only a small part of the Thunderbird's appeal. Power for the new Thunderbird was from a 292-cubic-inch V-8 that made the T-Bird a lively performer.

industry was quickly becoming a popular item in American car design. Fins were well on their way to growing up, out, and in any direction that would make the rear quarter look more aerodynamic. Anyone with an eye for style knew that something was going on, and that something was the noticeable growth of the fin as it took hold of the motoring public. Those that had entered the fin craze by merely adding on a bolted chrome trim piece now

had cause to retool with an integrated fin design. The public knew the real McCoy when they saw it, and a bolt-on fin just wouldn't do.

The industry fin leader Cadillac restyled in 1950, and although there were changes in front-end design as well as major trim upgrades, the small P-38–inspired tail treatment still reigned supreme on the rear quarter. The new 1950 Cadillac had a generally longer and lower appearance

Ford reintroduced the Continental in 1956 and although it was clearly a beautiful automobile, it lacked the huge fin that was becoming all the rage in the mid-1950s. Ford spared no expense in the Continental, and each one was delivered to the dealer in a fleece-lined canvas bag. A lofty price tag in the $10,000 range put the Continental out of reach of the average buyer, and the Continental Mark II would be phased out after only two years in production.

that was accented by sweeping lines on the entire body. The European racing circuit was aghast when American sportsman Briggs Cunningham entered two 1950 Cadillacs in the 24 Hours of Le Mans in 1950. Although one of the racers carried a relatively stock body, the other was an aerodynamic thoroughbred racer. The car was appropriately dubbed *"Le Monstre"* (The Monster) due to its massive size when compared to the nimble European road racers of the day. Cunningham's cars would

finish a respectable 10th and 11th thanks in part to Cadillac's 331-cubic-inch V-8.

The new lineup for Cadillac in 1950 saw the company quickly shedding its immediate postwar design and moving into the wonderful 1950s with lightning speed. If there was any doubt as to the fin's growing popularity, it was put to rest in 1950 when for the first time in its 48-year history, Cadillac sold more than 100,000 cars. Cadillac would celebrate its Golden Anniversary in 1952 with only

Pontiac featured a completely redesigned body for 1955 that spoke directly to the "more is better" theme of the 1950s. A huge divided bumper up front and twin "Silver Streak" bands set Pontiac apart from the competition. Wraparound windshields were also new for 1955 and made a significant contribution to the new streamlined look. Although the tailfin was still small, the stage was now set for the explosion of the large tailfin that would signify the 1950s.

a minor face-lift, but the P-38–inspired tailfins were still an intricate part of the Cadillac look. The P-38 inspiration would be seen all the way into 1956, but as evidenced by the Eldorado in 1955, Cadillac's fin would play a much more important role for the 1957 lineup.

The one aspect of automobile design that GM designer Harley Earl aimed for was a clear identity among the different makes. This accounts for some of the design features found on GM's postwar line-up. Pontiac featured an Indian-head hood ornament, while Cadillac carried a chrome V on the

33

Pontiac's Silver Streak styling theme carried through the entire length of the car ending with an elegant tailfin that gave a slight hint of things to come. GM's use of two-tone colors again made for an attractive automobile that the public loved. Pontiac would rank sixth in the industry with a calendar year production of 581,860 units.

Although the design for Plymouth's 1955 lineup was already in place, a last-minute change by Chrysler stylist Virgil Exner resulted in a car that was right at home in the mid-1950s. The new design by Exner allowed Plymouth to cross the line into the modern postwar look of the 1950s with ease. The wild tailfin treatment was only a few short years away, and Plymouth would be ready. Plymouth produced 8,473 Belvedere convertibles like the one pictured here.

hood and deck lid. There were also signature rocket-shaped taillight lenses and a streamlined, aerodynamic, jet-inspired hood ornament found on the Oldsmobile. A fascinating story lies behind the porthole treatment that was a mainstay of Buick for many years. It seems that the head of Buick's design studio, Ned Nickles, was convinced by Joe Funk, one of his modelers, to try something unique on his new 1948 Buick Roadmaster Convertible. Funk cut three holes in the Buick's front fenders, then installed lights that flashed in synchronization with the spark plugs. The effect was mesmerizing, and when Buick's Executive Vice President Harlow Curtice noticed the cutouts, he insisted that the

design become standard on the 1949 Buick. The dies were retooled and the final result was the signature portholes that became Buick's most recognizable feature for many years to come.

This was the way things were done in the styling studios of the day. In an age long before the advent of computer-aided design, cars were designed by a simple method involving the human hand, a hand often dried out from working with clay or stiff from holding a pencil. There was also the input of many talented people, but the process had a pecking order that defined what the ultimate design would be. At GM, if Harley Earl didn't like it, it was unlikely to become a final design.

Plymouth's tailfin treatment for 1955 was sheer beauty in motion. A linear edge that ran the car's length culminated in a large oval pod that housed the taillight. The whole package resulted in a smooth design that the motoring public loved. Two-tone color treatments added to the appeal of Plymouth's offerings for 1955.

Dodge jumped into the fin wars with both feet in 1956. Although the 1956 Dodge lineup was largely a carryover from the previous year, a big, beautiful tailfin became an intricate part of the rear quarter panel. Dodge was also nursing the beginning of the musclecar era with a multitude of V-8 engines available up to 295 horsepower. Dodge would win 11 NASCAR events in 1956, proving that horsepower was a serious issue. Push-button automatic shifting was also a big hit, and Dodge would post a production of 233,686 cars for the model year.

Although many designers were rubbing their chins in the early and mid-1950s, conservative styling still stood as the hallmark of Ford's lineup. The introduction of the Thunderbird in 1955 gave the public an impressive look into the new idea of an American sports car. Although it was initially billed as such, many Europeans balked at the idea of an American sports car. No, it may not have handled like the Jaguar XK 140, but it looked great and featured a 292-cubic-inch V-8 that propelled the 2,980-pound T-Bird with ease. While Ford was certainly aware of the fins' gaining popularity during the early 1950s, they chose the theme of planned obsolescence as the introductory Thunderbird fea-

While Dodge placed a heavy emphasis on horsepower for 1956, there was no doubt that the company was in the fin wars for good. Dodge's fins had grown taller and more aerodynamic and left little doubt as to the company's intentions. Fin treatment was one of the few upgrades for Dodge in 1956 as strong sales in 1955 called for only a minor face-lift.

The 1953 model year would be Oldsmobile's last body style to carry the immediate postwar look. The Series 98 Holiday two-door hardtop was an attractive automobile that proved very popular with the motoring public. Its small but protruding tailfin was accented by chrome and ended with a rocket-inspired taillight. The Holiday Hardtop was a heavy car at 3,906 pounds, but power from its 303-cubic-inch V-8 was more than enough to move it along. Oldsmobile captured nine NASCAR events in 1953.

tured a low-keyed rear quarter treatment that was both stylish and tasteful. While its competitor, the Corvette, withered on the vine for lack of sales, the Thunderbird gained unheard-of popularity and would spend the 1950s in a steady state of development that saw its fins grow just a bit each year.

In contrast, the Corvette would shed its rocket-inspired pod on the rear quarter for a smooth look on the 1956 model. The Corvette would spend the 1950s in stark defiance of the fin phenomenon and in the end would pay dearly as the Thunderbird would outsell it hands down. There were some experimental fins grafted onto the Corvette, but none of these would ever reach the production stage. Instead, the public either accepted or rejected the finless fiberglass wonder from Chevrolet. Of course the Corvette would have the last laugh as prices for the early-model Corvette have climbed astronomically in recent years.

The Corvette would not be the only automobile to attempt to defy the oncoming roar of the fin. On October 16, 1954, William Clay Ford announced that Ford had created a Continental Division and was about to release a whole new version of Edsel's original design. Although it certainly was a beautiful car, more attention was paid to maintaining the roots of the original design than to the demand for the fin. When Ford introduced the Continental Mark II in 1956, it was clearly an about-face of the accepted design practice of the day. Again, Ford can be credited with a tasteful design while maintaining supreme elegance. The

It might have been the Lockheed F-104 Starfighter or the Grumman F-9F Cougar that provided the inspiration for Oldsmobile's hood mascot, but the jetlike chrome piece mounted on the hood left little doubt as to where GM was going. The sleek chromium mascot would point the way on several Oldsmobile models over the next few years. Oldsmobile would play a prominent part in the fin wars as its designs of the late 1950s would be as wild as any that roamed the streets at the time.

A complete restyle for Oldsmobile in 1954 saw the company move into the mid-1950s with a clear vision of the future. A new longer and lower look set the stage for the coming fin wars. Its fin remained little more than a taillight pod, but it still carried its jet plane hood mascot up front. Oldsmobile's new crisp and clean styling helped the company capture fourth place in industry output with a total of 433,810 units for the calendar year.

company also went to great lengths to ensure that the Mark II had no equal in terms of quality and craftsmanship. Each engine was dynamometer-tested and then torn down for inspection before installation. All bolts used in its assembly were of aircraft grade, and all wheel and tire assemblies were precision-balanced by hand. The Mark II was shipped to dealers in a fleece-lined canvas bag. While it was a hit at the Paris Auto Show when introduced on October 6, 1955, its design was most definitely

Although Cadillac's 1956 Eldorado featured a fin signifying the company's future designs, the Coupe DeVille still carried the P-38–inspired tailfin from 1948. Cadillac's cars had grown longer and heavier, but their smooth and graceful lines were right at home in the mid-1950s. Nineteen fifty-six would be the last year of the original fin design as all Cadillacs would be accented with a new longer and taller fin design for the coming year. The stage was now set for the very pinnacle of the fin's dominance in American car design.

acting in defiance of the accepted practice of the day. No wild fin treatment, no excessive use of chrome, and a lofty price tag in the $10,000 range put the Mark II in a league of its own. In a clear demonstration of the fin's popularity, the Mark II would bow out after only two years of production. Ford would produce a mere 2,996 Mark IIs, and in an ironic twist of fate the Oakland Boulevard assembly plant that built the Mark II would retool for production of the new Edsel. Lincoln would completely restyle with the Mark III in 1958 and it would bear little resemblance to the Continental Mark II.

Many car builders were still using a conservative approach to the fin in the mid-1950s. While many were still developing their new designs in the early 1950s, hostilities overseas again began to cause a ripple effect on the American car market. When the North Korean army invaded South Korea on June 25, 1950, many already knew that it was just a matter of time before the conflict spread. With the fate of the free world once again at stake, the United States again found itself in a war against communism. The war effort demanded new and better munitions, and the U.S. government turned to Detroit as the United States again began tooling up for the war effort. While its size and scope would not reach the proportions of World War II, the retooling did have an impact on Detroit. Cadillac continued to build tanks while many other car builders built various other components for the conflict.

Although the war siphoned off some of Detroit's industrial capacity, it also gave impetus for the development of a new generation of jet-powered aircraft. This new generation of jets would prove to be inspirational in the design of the American automobile. Of course, developmental work on jet-powered aircraft had taken place for some time, but the Korean War proved that the United States needed a fast and agile fighter plane. This need gave rise to a new breed of sleek jets that had one thing in common, a more aerodynamic design than anything the world had previously seen. This slippery new look would not be lost in Detroit as the tailfin and many other trim pieces began to resemble some of this new breed of aircraft. Jets such as the Lockheed F-80 Shooting Star and the F-94 Starfire were inspirational in the new look of the automobile. With power measured in terms of thrust and speeds reaching previously unheard-of proportions, the jet age was proving to be the driving force in American car design. Of course there were other indirect factors driving American aviation efforts during the early 1950s,

not the least of which was the Soviet Union's introduction of the MiG-9. This early jet-powered fighter caused great concern in the U.S. Air Force, and companies such as Lockheed, North American, and Grumman scrambled to fill contracts from the U.S. government for new and better jets. Overall, the early 1950s would see an incredible effort in the development of new and better jets for the nation's defense. While the average American couldn't own one of these new jets, they could have a fender spear or a jet hood mascot on their new car.

When hostilities in Korea ended in the summer of 1953, the United States was once again at peace. With the lessons of aerodynamics learned from the steadily developing jet age, Detroit's designers could now turn their attention to the automobile. Designers such as Harley Earl and Virgil Exner began to push their designers for new and faster-looking cars that would satisfy the nation's need for speed. The direction of Cadillac's future design completely changed in 1952 when a talented young designer named Dave Holls joined Cadillac's design staff and quickly began work under the direction of Harley Earl. It was Holls who designed the ultimate finned warrior as he created the 1959 Cadillac tailfin that would serve as the defining fin of the 1950s. Holls spent his career at the design studios of General Motors and turned out some of Detroit's most fascinating automobiles.

The general growth of the fin is easily traced through marques such as Oldsmobile. As one of the original founders of the automobile itself, GM had no intention of letting its other divisions just stand by as the fin grabbed hold of the American public. For 1953, Oldsmobile offered a wonderful array of cars that clearly indicated the direction that Olds was taking. Riding on the Ninety-Eight

Chevrolet's Bel Air two-door hardtop for 1956 was a minor face-lift from the previous year, but with two-tone paint schemes and fender skirts it rode into the mid-1950s with style. Chevrolet's 1956 lineup would prove to be a winner and the company would become the nation's number one automaker with calendar-year sales of 1,621,004 units. The 1956 lineup came in a multitude of body styles with the two-door Nomad station wagon being the most expensive. The small but elegant tailfin was right at home on the 1956 lineup, but would grow even more the following year.

Series, the Holiday two-door hardtop was a handsome car that featured a long rear deck accented by two taillight pods on the rear quarter. A better indicator of the future was up front as the hood mascot was a beautiful jet-inspired chrome piece flanked by two simulated jet engines pointing the

way. Oldsmobile was emphasizing its racing activities and was a favorite winner at many NASCAR tracks. Overall, Oldsmobile captured nine checkered flags at NASCAR events in 1953, including Buck Baker's win at the Southern 500. For 1954, Oldsmobile restyled and had completely shed its rounded look of the late 1940s. The tailfin was little more than a rounded pod for its taillight, but the Oldsmobile jet still stood guard on the hood. A slight restyle of the tailfin for 1956 saw the rear quarter panel receiving a more sculptured look that spoke loudly to the fin movement. Although the quintessential finned Oldsmobile was still a few model years away, a close look at Oldsmobile's designs in the preceding years of the late 1950s shows how the fin was creeping up and crawling into the hearts of the American motorist.

As Chrysler entered the 1950s, a movement was under way in the company to build smaller cars. This was in response to several marketing surveys that said the public wanted smaller cars. The marketing people must have had to look hard for people who wanted these cars since this was certainly not the case. As Chrysler entered the 1953 model year, both Plymouth and Dodge had shed an average of 670 pounds over the previous year. They were also visually smaller than the traditional Ford, Pontiac, or Chevrolet. The downsizing resulted in the loss of a substantial portion of Chrysler's market share. Clearly, something had to be done. The answer came from the legendary Virgil Exner, who in the space of 18 months managed to redesign Chrysler's entire lineup for 1955. The result was a longer and lower car that propelled all four marques from the Chrysler camp to great success. Plymouth's 1955 Belvedere convertible featured a longer and lower body that quickly brought it up to par with the competition. Although Plymouth's fin for 1955 lacked the vertical height that would become the hallmark of fin design, it did make ideal use of a streamlined taillight, and a restyle in 1956 would see the addition of a genuine tailfin. As Dodge made clear in 1956, the folks at Mopar were not about to be left behind in the fin wars. A large, sweeping fin with

its taillights set vertically was just what the motoring public was looking for. DeSoto featured a stunning design for 1955 that proved that Mopar would not be outdone in the design department. Once again the aerodynamic, jet-inspired design was in vogue as Mopar's 1956 lineup would be very successful. As we shall see later on, Chrysler would draw a line in the sand with its 1957 models, which would turn out to be some of the most beautiful cars of the day.

With the postwar market's insatiable appetite for new automobiles quickly becoming filled, Detroit drifted into the mid-1950s with a renewed sense of competition. The independents were struggling to keep up with the well-capitalized Big Three. Although many were already on their deathbeds, there would be several efforts to defy the odds and survive. The mid-1950s would see several mergers that meant a few more years in the market for some, and certain death for others. While this struggle was a gallant one, the ranks of the car builders would thin considerably in the next decade.

By the mid-1950s, the stage was set for the explosion of the fin. Even though there was certainly an attractive look to the rounded taillight pod, Detroit would soon find out that it was not enough. The next several years witnessed a sharp increase in the fin's height as well as its length. No longer would a slight fin be grafted onto the automobile; the automobile itself would be built around the tailfin. While the public would flock to it in droves, they would also catch a glimpse of many of Detroit's dreams. As we shall see in the next chapter, the fins of the 1950s were predominant on the production automobile, but the real fin craze was found in the design studios of Detroit. Yes, the fin was here to stay, and it was about to head into outer space.

3

Detroit Goes Wild

If the general public thought that the fin was becoming excessive, one look at the New York or Chicago Auto Shows in the mid-1950s gave the consumer a strong indication that the best was yet to come. While the fin was quickly entering its renaissance period during the mid-1950s, there were many ideas locked up in Detroit's design studios that would prove that America's love affair with the fin was not over yet.

The 1956 Firebird II took a different direction from its predecessor. While it was still gas turbine–powered, it featured seating for four and was much larger than the Firebird I. Aircraft inspiration is clearly evident once again as demonstrated by the turbine-inspired air intakes up front. The Firebird II still delights crowds today as shown here on display at the 1996 Meadowbrook Concours. Don Keefe

The Cadillac La Espada was one of three custom-built show cars for the 1954 General Motors Motorama. The La Espada rode on a 115-inch wheelbase and featured a fiberglass body. The future was foretold in many of the La Espada's design features, which included a sharply raked 60-degree windshield and superfins that would show up on production-model Cadillacs in just a few years. The name "La Espada" would never find its way onto a production-based Cadillac, but its design features were a clear indication of the future. National Automotive History Collection, Detroit Public Library

Even though many dream cars would prove to be mere thoughts of fantasy, some did give rise to many interesting ideas that found their way onto the production-based cars of the day. Concept cars that carried the banner for their respective companies on the show circuit were actually built for more than just show. Many of them served as rolling test beds to gauge the public's opinion on various design features. This enabled the car builders of Detroit to effectively measure the public's opinion without endangering sales of an all-new car. While some concept cars were built for nothing more than show, many others were built only as scale model mock-ups. In any case, our study of the wonderful

fin would not be complete without taking a glimpse at Detroit's dream machines.

If dream cars are created by thought, then clay is the medium through which they are expressed. Within the safe confines of the various manufacturers' special project design studios, modelers were free to test the limits of style and taste. To be sure, most of the experimental work would never see the light of day in terms of production. After all, the American public loved something new, but there is a big difference between something different and something new. A good case in point was the introduction of the Edsel in 1958. Other than the usual teething problems associated with a new car,

Cadillac's experimental show car for 1959 was the XP-74 Cadillac Cyclone. The design influence of the fin is clearly evident, as the Cyclone seemed to be straight out of a science fiction movie. The Cyclone was built with several gadgets that dazzled the general public. The car was equipped with a power-operated rear-hinged bubble canopy that opened and closed for exit and entry. The two missile-inspired pods up front housed a proximity warning system that informed the driver of impending hazards. Note the lower skeg moldings that would later show up on the 1961 production-based Cadillac. Bud Juneau collection

there was nothing mechanically wrong with the Edsel, it merely had a new and different look. However, the "horse collar" front-end treatment was simply more than the public could take and it did not sell well. Buick also experienced sales problems when it introduced an all-new look for 1959. While it was clearly keeping pace with the fin movement, it proved to be much more than conservative Buick buyers could handle. The result was a disastrous sales year for the company. While the fin had crept into the hearts of the motoring public slowly, Ford's Edsel and Buick's new style had attempted to change the public's mind overnight.

Where does a dream car come from and how is it built? The answer to these questions lies in the hearts and minds of the designers. Men such as Virgil Exner, Harley Earl, Dick Teague, Dave Holls, and Gil Spear were men of vision who wielded a powerful pencil in the car-building industry. After all, the automobile's reliability had been proven some decades before. By the 1950s, the average American family could simply jump into the sedan and head for the open road. The need to bring along a trunk full of spare tires or engine parts had passed some years before. The nation's highways were smooth and a service sta-

The beautiful X-1000 was designed at the request of Ford's vice president and general manager of styling George Walker, shown here with a 3/8-scale model of the design. The X-1000 was designed by Ford designer Alex Tremulis at Ford's Advanced Studio during 1955–1956. Man's fascination with space travel is clearly evident as even its fins were retractable. While it certainly was interesting to look at, no body panels from the X-1000 would show up on any production-based Ford. From the Collections of Henry Ford Museum & Greenfield Village

tion was just around the corner. With dependability a proven science, the design of the automobile could now take center stage. A close look at the postwar marketing campaign of any given car builder usually reveals only passing remarks on reliability. Indeed it was the style, color, and other visual cues that attempted to sell the latest model.

So it was that Detroit would build its dream cars. These are the cars that didn't make it to the production stage, but caused a major stir on the show circuits. The sky was the limit on these special automobiles that were built not for sheer numbers, but existed only to see how far the design stu-

dios could go. Of course some components would reach the streets of America. Perhaps a headlight here or a tailfin there, but overall, dream cars allowed the public to do just that, dream. Maybe the average car buyer couldn't have the Ford FX-Atmos sitting in their driveway, but a Fairlane 500 Skyliner was certainly a possibility.

Although dream cars of the 1950s with their aircraft-styled fins and rocket nose cone front ends made everyone look twice, many were little more than mock-ups. With bodies molded of fiberglass, clay, and aluminum, dream cars were usually put together in a very short amount of time. Some

Ford's design studios were alive with energy during the 1950s and nothing was beyond the scope of the designer's pencil. This drawing of the 1954 Exploratta is an indication of just how far Ford went in the studio. Resembling more of a rocket than a car, the general public was left to decide its source of power, as turbine, electric, or nuclear were all possibilities. The Exploratta clearly defines the limits of the fin movement as the design studios of Detroit were letting their imaginations run wild during the height of the fin craze. From the Collections of Henry Ford Museum & Greenfield Village

were built without engines, leaving the general public to guess if it was going to be gas turbine–powered, electric-, or maybe even nuclear-powered. Others were built in miniature in order to see what their final form would look like. Some scale-model concept cars were even motorized with small engines and operated by radio control to enable the designers to see what they looked like while in motion. Whatever its size or power,

the dream car lived only to inspire the automotive public and it usually did just that, although only for a short time. The sad truth is that many dream cars were scrapped after serving on the tour circuit for a year or two. Some did survive and continue to delight all who are able to catch a glimpse of these incredible machines that are kept in the vaults of various museums and collections today. It is only fitting that interest in the dream

The Ford FX-Atmos was built as a rolling showcase of Ford's superfuturistic concept of the automobile. The FX-Atmos was a big hit at the 1954 Chicago Auto Show and the general public couldn't get enough of the wonderful show cars of Detroit's fancy. The FX-Atmos was built only as a fiberglass show car and had no supporting structure. Sadly, by the mid-1960s, the car began to sag and its Plexiglas roof began to discolor. It was then broken up, although a small model of the car still exists today. Note the aircraft-inspired tailfins. From the Collections of Henry Ford Museum & Greenfield Village

car concept would reach its heyday in the thick of the fin wars of the 1950s.

Credit for the dream car concept can be given to Harley Earl, whose influence and charisma wielded a considerable amount of power at General Motors. Indeed, Earl's power at GM caused many to tremble at the mention of his name. He worked long hours and demanded that everyone who worked for him do the same. Much of Earl's charisma originated from his early years spent at GM's La Salle and Cadillac divisions. GM had recruited Earl for the design of the 1927 La Salle

and his resulting effort shocked the automotive world. Never before had such stunning lines of European influence been seen on an American production-based vehicle. The 1927 La Salle put Earl's name on the map in automotive design. With his success firmly planted on his first attempt at a production vehicle, it is easy to imagine the influence he had gained at GM by the 1950s. Indeed, the legend of Harley Earl is still talked of in Detroit today. The General Motors Motorama Auto Shows enabled Earl to start his design work with a blank sheet of paper. No

The Lincoln Futura was one of the fortunate dream cars built as a running automobile. The Futura was the brainchild of Lincoln's head of styling, Bill Schmidt. The design is clearly aircraft inspired as evidenced by the twin jet–styled canopies and fins both fore and aft. Schmidt claimed that the design was also inspired by tropical sea life as evidenced by the sharklike features on the front end. The Futura would go on to achieve fame in Hollywood as the Batmobile, *created by George Barris.* From the Collections of Henry Ford Museum & Greenfield Village

longer reworks of an old design, the Motorama cars of the 1950s were outrageous and showed the public what a car could look like when crossed with a rocket.

Harley Earl and Dave Holls' work at Cadillac would give the public some eye-catching designs during the fin craze of the 1950s. One of Cadillac's first entries into the 1953 Motorama Auto Show was the LeMans. The LeMans featured many styling cues that ended up in production, including its entire front end, which would show up on Cadillac's 1954 models. The two-seater fiberglass roadster featured a hooded headlight that would find its way onto Cadillac's 1954 and 1957 production cars. The GM Motorama show of 1954 saw the introduction of Cadillac's La Espada and the

El Camino. Both of these cars were as wild and different as concept cars could be. The El Camino's rear fin would turn up on the 1955 Eldorado and that same fin would become the mainstay of Cadillac's 1958 lineup.

For 1955, Cadillac resurrected the name of Earl's famous creation, the La Salle. While introducing many innovations in automotive design, the La Salle show cars broke from the tradition of the fin and instead chose a smaller and more conservative design that seemed to defy the fin craze. The 1955 La Salle roadster rebelled against the trend of the day even more as its back end appeared to be cut off at the rear wheel. Both La Salle concept cars featured a cut-out behind the front wheel that would later show up on the Corvette.

As the last of GM's trio of gas turbine–powered cars, the Firebird III was a finned wonder that was all jet. Its tall vertical fins and twin-canopy design made it look more at home in the air than on the road. The Firebird III featured a multitude of fins adorning its entire body. All of the Firebird prototypes were featured as Motorama show cars and generated much excitement from the public. From the National Automotive History Collection, Detroit Public Library

At the height of the fin wars in 1959, Cadillac had gone ballistic with a concept car called the Cyclone. While many Motorama show cars openly carried an aircraft-inspired theme, the Cyclone borrowed its cues directly from man's quest to reach the stars. Its front end featured a pair of rocket nose cones, which housed a radar system that warned the driver of any obstacles in its path. Of course its rocket pods would have torpedoed anything in its path anyway, but it was a hit in 1959. The Cyclone's tailfin treatment was even more radical with two vertical stabilizers equaling the height of its bubble-styled canopy. The Cyclone definitely took the fin concept to the

limit, and one can only wonder what it might have looked like shooting down the streets of America.

Several show cars made it into production. The car known as the legendary American sports car is one of those that had a life after the show circuit. The Chevrolet Corvette made its public debut at the New York Auto Show in January 1953. There are many legendary stories of the Corvette's rocky start, one of which is its signature crossed-flags emblem. The Corvette's identification flags were actually changed on the night before the show. The original design featured an American flag—but someone realized that it is forbidden by law to use the American flag for promotional

Chrysler would enlist the help of Italian body builder Ghia for its contribution to the finned dream cars of the 1950s. This artist's rendering of the 1957 Chrysler Dart shows the smooth and balanced lines of the aerodynamic creation from Ghia. The Ghia's body panels were hand beaten by the superior craftsmen of Ghia at its plant in Turin, Italy. Power for the Ghia came from a 375-horsepower 300-C Hemi. Dr. Paul Sable collection

purposes. The Corvette's crossed-flag emblem was redesigned in time for the show and the rest is history. While the Corvette was introduced as a dream car, public reaction was so strong that it was rushed into production. The result was a car that leaked around its windows and quite simply didn't run very well due to the complexity of its multi-carbureted engine. Indeed the Corvette almost died a quiet death until it was saved by the most unlikely of saviors. The Ford Thunderbird's introduction in 1955 meant that GM had to continue production of the Corvette or abandon the two-seater market. While the Thunderbird outsold the Corvette in its early years, the Corvette did eventually reach a profitable status for GM.

The Corvette proved to be a wonderful inspiration for GM's show cars of the 1950s, but in stark defiance of the fin wars, its rear quarter treatment featured rounded lines that were tasteful and elegant. In 1954, Chevy introduced the Nomad to a delighted public. Its Corvette-inspired front end and two-door wagon concept featured a rocket-style pod in its fin. There was also a beautiful fastback Corvette–inspired car for 1954 called the Corvair. In keeping with the General Motors tradition, Chevrolet always tested a car's name before giving it an official design. Thus the Biscayne of 1955 and the Impala of 1956 were both hits on the Motorama show circuit. The Biscayne featured a double wrap-around windshield and concave door panels heading

Built by Ghia for Chrysler, the aerodynamic Ghia Gilda was the star of the 1955 Turin Show. The Gilda was a masterpiece in terms of its streamlined elegance. Its construction was aluminum over a steel frame and it featured such unusual styling tricks as partly concealed wheels and huge tailfins. Top speed for the Gilda was said to be 140 miles per hour. Dr. Paul Sable collection

toward the rear of the car. Strangely enough, Chevrolet's dream cars of the mid-1950s completely shunned the fin movement. Perhaps Chevrolet was already preparing itself for the ultimate demise of the fin. In any event, the XP 700 made its debut in 1958 as the personal car of Bill Mitchell, head of GM styling. This Corvette became a test bed for many innovations of the Corvette in future years. Vents, side coves, trim lines, and side pipes were all hung onto the XP 700 at one time or another. The 1958 XP 700 became such an interesting project that it was used as a show car for 1959. As the Corvette eased into the 1960s it would enjoy a strong appeal on the dream car circuit. There were several versions of what Corvette called the Mako Shark as well as testing for building the Corvette with midengine

power, but the fin would never become an intricate part of the Corvette's design.

While the design work on Ford's production-based automobiles would always carry a tasteful use of chrome and conservative fin height, the company's dream cars were some of the most outrageous Detroit would produce. Indeed, Ford's concept cars were the product of pure fantasy, as its tailfins would rival that of any fighter plane in existence at the time. While the designers at Ford were acutely aware of the fin's climbing popularity, the early 1950s found the company deeply engrossed in the development of a retractable hardtop.

The genesis of this idea actually started in 1948 when Ford Advanced Studio Stylist Gil Spear heard rumors of Buick's new 1949 Riviera hardtop convertible. Spear thought that the Buick was marketing its new model on false advertising, as the top didn't actually retract in the true convertible sense. Back at his studio, Spear began work on a concept car that would ultimately test the retractable concept and become known as the Syrtis. The idea would be tossed around at Ford for a few years, but a model of the Syrtis would begin life based on the dimensions of the 1952 Ford. Here again man's fascination with outer space would play a significant role. Spear designed the Syrtis with a space ship theme that started at the front with a streamlined nose and ended with the telltale fins that were now influencing American car design.

By 1955, Ford's use of the fin on their production vehicles was still in its infancy, but back at the design studios the fin was reaching for the stars. Ford stylist Alex Tremulis designed the X-1000 during 1955–1956. The X-1000 was a pure flight of fancy. While many concept cars forecasted a significant design concept that would later appear on a production-based car, the X-1000 was a pure dream. The only components of the X-1000 that would see the production line were a few instrument panel knobs. A streamlined car by any standards, the X-1000 featured smooth lines and a huge set of fins that actually retracted into the body. The X-1000 was also designed to use a rear-mounted gas-turbine engine and it was campaigned extensively on the auto show circuit. A live display at the Chicago Auto Show featured several Ford modelers deeply engrossed in building a clay mock-up of the X-1000. This gave the general public a firsthand look at how the design studios actually worked.

One of Ford's more popular concept cars was the FX-Atmos. Built for the 1954 Chicago Auto Show, the FX-Atmos caused quite a stir. Its low-slung body accented by twin rocket pod nose cones and a wild fin treatment was second to none in the show car circuit. Its futuristic design spoke loudly to the space travel theme that was all the rage in the 1950s. The FX-Atmos was a true concept car as it never had an engine and was built purely for the public to look at. The FX-Atmos in its show form that the public saw was a fiberglass mock-up that was built by Creative Industries and took about three months to build. The entire body was molded in one piece as a solid unit; as such, the doors, trunk, and hood did not open. Its Plexiglas canopy was molded as a separate unit with a removable center section. In order for one to experience the interior of the FX-Atmos, the center section was removed and passengers were lifted in by a crane. The FX-Atmos earned its keep on the show circuit dazzling many who saw it. Sadly, by the mid-1960s its unsupported fiberglass body began to sag and it was destroyed.

Another winged warrior of the Ford show car phenomena was the Lincoln Futura. The Futura was the idea of Lincoln's head stylist, Bill Schmidt. The most unusual aspect of the Futura was its inspiration. While most of the dream cars were looking exclusively to the stars for their aerodynamic lines, the Futura took its cues from tropical sea life. The story goes that Schmidt was vacationing in the Bahamas in 1952 when a diving encounter with a shark gave him the inspiration for the Futura's design. The sharklike fins on the Futura are clearly evident from all angles. Nevertheless, the design influence of the jet era was also clearly evident in the Futura's futuristic body.

Lincoln selected Ghia of Italy to build the Futura and it was constructed in just three months at a cost of $75,000. It arrived in the United States just in time for the Chicago Auto Show on January 8, 1955. The Futura then toured the show circuit with stops in Detroit and New York. Its twin

Another beautiful creation from Ghia built for DeSoto was the Flight-Sweep I. An electrically operated convertible top and fully operational electric side windows were just a few of the luxuries built into the Flight-Sweep I. While many of Detroit's car builders would use their own studios, Chrysler relied heavily on Ghia for the creation of its dream cars. Dr. Paul Sable collection

canopy roof, huge jetlike tailfins, and simulated jetlike air intakes both fore and aft are the quintessential components of a 1950s show car. Even better was the fact that the Futura was one of the lucky show cars to actually be built as a running automobile. The Futura was truly a remarkable dream car that went on to lead a fascinating life. After its completion on the show circuit, the Futura

wound up in the hands of Hollywood car builder George Barris, who turned it into one of Hollywood's most famous cars, known as the *Batmobile*.

If Ford's dream cars were bordering on the outrageous, then the folks at GM were definitely going above and beyond the stratosphere. In 1954, GM introduced the Firebird I at the GM Motorama Auto Show. While its original design was never intended to become a production automobile, its name would surface on Dick Teague's rework of Chevrolet's Camaro for Pontiac in 1967. The Firebird I truly tested the design limits of the day. Resembling more of a rocket than an automobile, the Firebird I was powered by a 379-horsepower gas turbine engine. Several manufacturers would experiment with turbine power, but none would ever reach the production stage. GM would continue with the Firebird prototype design and would also build the Firebird II and the Firebird III. While the Firebird II began to resemble something that might actually reach the American public's driveway, the Firebird III headed directly to the stars. Looking more like something from a NASA launch pad, the Firebird III was as wild as a tailfin could ever get. Multiple use of the vertical stabilizer theme was evident in several places on the Firebird III. While certainly not practical, the Firebird III did introduce a few innovations that would eventually see the light of day. Cruise control, an antiskid braking system, and automatic headlamps were only a few of the features that would eventually find their way onto the regular-production automobile.

Not to be left out, Chrysler chose a different avenue in pursuit of their dream creations. In 1949 Chrysler President K. T. Keller hired Virgil Exner. While he may not have known it at the time, Keller had just solidified Chrysler's design direction for the next generation. Keller made Exner Director of Advanced Styling in his own studio that was known as Chrysler Styling. Within the solitude of his studio and without the pressure of production-car designs, Exner worked on Chrysler's dream cars. A visit from Italian coachbuilder Carrozzeria Ghia resulted in a series of dream cars that held an extensive European influence. In particular, the Ghia-built Dart of 1957 is a finned wonder of beautifully crafted lines.

Another beauty of Exner's dream car designs met with a sad fate. Completed after 15 months of intense labor at the Ghia facility, the car known as the *1956 Norseman* was loaded into the cargo hold of the *Andrea Doria*. The ship sank after a collision with the Swedish liner *Stockholm* and the beautiful Norseman was lost. Sadly, it now entertains nothing more than passing fish swimming by.

The fabulous 1950s would see some of the wildest fins to ever grace the roadways and exhibition halls. While they never reached the driveways of the American public, they allowed everyone's imagination to fly a little higher. What was the fate of these wonderful creations from Detroit's imagination? Sadly, many were destroyed after their useful display years were played out. Some were saved and these wonderful artifacts are among the most treasured possessions of the museums and collections that house them. The automobile has served a number of purposes over the years, but the concept cars were not built to haul around the family or make the neighborhood milk deliveries; they existed only to test and entertain our imaginations. To be certain, Detroit has not abandoned the concept car theory, but the wild fins and groundbreaking ideas of the 1950s have given way to computer-generated images of what the automobile might be like in the future. The concept car of the 1950s, with its obvious use of the infant jet-age style and tailfins that reached for the stars, remains locked in a time of innocence and grandeur.

Battle Lines are Drawn

A s the late 1950s emerged, design and style were reaching a new level of influence in manufacturing. Everything from the automobile to the toaster was taking on a completely new look, which spoke of streamlined elegance and often gave the impression of movement while sitting still. This design feature was mainly the result of the nation's quest for speed as the aviation industry continued to make great strides in aircraft design.

Representing one of Cadillac's best for 1959, the beautiful Eldorado Biarritz convertible featured vast amounts of chrome and a powerful 345-horsepower V-8 engine that propelled the 5,060-pound finned wonder with ease. Americans looking for fuel economy would have to look elsewhere, as the 1959 Cadillac was built for beauty and style. Cadillac would assemble 142,272 cars in 1959, dominating the U.S. luxury car market.

61

A competitor in name only, the Imperial was a quality-built automobile that spared no expense in comfort. Riding on a huge 129-inch wheelbase, the Imperial was well suited for a night on the town. Sharp styling with finely sculptured lines made the Imperial a standout in the crowd. Quality control was a hallmark of the Imperial's image as each car was checked and rechecked for fit and finish. Despite its beauty and luxury, its rival Cadillac would outsell the Imperial by a wide margin.

America was also becoming infatuated with space exploration. The jet engine and the rocket were redefining the science of aerodynamics and this research would not be lost in Detroit's design of the automobile.

At the forefront of streamlined aircraft design work were companies such as Lockheed and Grumman. As the nation's premier builders of the new generation of jet-powered aircraft, these companies knew how to build a sleek and slippery design that seemed to defy the laws of gravity. The Lockheed F-104 Starfighter, under development since 1952, proved itself when it entered service in 1958. The F-104 was a needle-nosed aircraft that was able to attain a level speed of 1,400 miles per hour, and climb to 15.15 miles in about 4.5 minutes. The press dubbed the F-104 "the missile with a man in it." When the first production Grumman F-9F Cougar took to the skies on January 18, 1954, its Pratt & Whitney J48-P-8 turbojet engine was pushing

Representing the top of the line for DeSoto in 1959, the Adventurer convertible featured a wide array of trim features that literally defined the 1950s. DeSoto's triple taillight theme was an outstanding example of the classic fin design that was so prominent in the 1950s. DeSoto would build only 97 Adventurer convertibles for 1959, making this example a truly rare automobile. Heavy use of gold anodizing made the Adventurer shine.

out 8,500 pounds of thrust. The F-9F's top speed of 705 miles per hour was unheard of in a piston-powered aircraft, but these were the days of the jet engine. While the general public could only dream of such blinding speeds, they could get the feel and look of the modern jet with any one of the aviation-inspired creations from Detroit.

As automobile design entered the late 1950s, it was clearly evident that everyone had caught on to industry leader Cadillac's fin; however, Cadillac was still showing everyone the path to follow. The 1948 model with its P-38 aircraft–inspired tailfin had set a precedent that Cadillac had cultivated into complete success. Beginning in the mid-1950s, Cadillac raised the bar just a bit each year until its fins gave the impression of flight. Cadillac easily maintained its status as a trendsetter because of the ever-thinning car market of the late 1950s. The once mighty Packard was operating on life support, and Lincoln was still trying to figure things

Full-size Fords for 1959 utilized a tasteful design of the fin that was graceful and stylish. A focused effort on building a production model with a fully retractable hardtop roof had paid off with a novelty that no one else had. In a time of excess and chrome overload, Ford can be credited with using tasteful restraint in its use of the fin. Production-line Fords would never see the gargantuan proportions of the competition, but Ford's design studios would know no limits in their use of the fin.

out after dropping the Continental Mark II. The Lincoln Mark III would join its sister models the Capri and Premier and offer a fin with a long, sweeping body that would bear no resemblance whatsoever to its predecessor. Chrysler's Imperial, while proclaiming the last word in luxury and quality, was not catching on with the general public. In fact, production numbers for the Imperial didn't

even come close to Cadillac. This allowed Cadillac to enter the golden era of the fin unchallenged in its command of the luxury car market. With the competition searching for its place, Cadillac took bold steps in its fin design. The rules were simple: big cars with as much chrome as the engine could pull and a tailfin that was as tall as the body would hold. While this may not sound like an exercise in

Perhaps no more beautiful than in its convertible body style, the 1957 Chevrolet Bel Air was right at home in the 1950s. Powered by Chevrolet's 265-cubic-inch V-8, the Bel Air was a spirited performer. The 1957 convertible would go on to become one of the most popular postwar collector cars in the world. Today, the 1957 Bel Air convertible commands a premium on the collector market that many would have thought impossible at its introduction. This example has been completely restored.

taste, the cars that originated from the very pinnacle of the fin era are some of the most wonderful designs to ever grace the roadways.

In 1957, Cadillac introduced a variant of one of its show cars that would impress the motoring public, especially those with money to burn. The Eldorado Brougham was based on Cadillac's 1955 Eldorado Brougham show car and featured advanced aircraft styling. Cadillac left no stone unturned in outfitting the Eldorado Brougham in luxurious comfort, which accounted for its whopping price of $13,000. Cadillac's fin had now grown immensely from its original 1948 design, but due to the length and lower profile of Cadillac's late-1950s style, its fin looked right at home. The general public loved the 1957 Cadillacs and

The sharp dorsal fin on the 1957 Chevrolet would prove to be a classic design that would represent one of the most memorable milestones of the fin era. Chevrolet produced this fin design for one year only as 1958 would bring a complete change. Chevrolet outsold its rival Ford by a mere 136 cars in the calendar year 1957, marking one of the closest races ever in the quest to be number one.

After grooming the fin for several years, Oldsmobile Introduced a jet-like fin in 1958. The Super 88 convertible was a heavy car weighing in at 4,217 pounds. Power came from Oldsmobile's 371-cubic-inch V-8 that generated 305 horsepower. Oldsmobile was in firm command of the medium-price-class market in 1958 and many buyers found good value in Oldsmobile. Sadly, the marque has now been added to the casualty list in the ever-thinning car market of the new millennium. Bud Juneau

the numbers proved it. Cadillac would sell 146,841 cars in 1957, placing the company ninth in industry sales for the second year in a row.

Cadillac's 1958 lineup was generally a carry-over from 1957. There were a few minor changes and the Brougham's interior received a bit more attention, but overall Cadillac chose to let the success of its cars sell themselves. While Cadillac's fins were selling well, its power up front was propelling the huge cars with ease. Cadillac's standard engine for 1958 was the 365-cubic-inch V-8,

which generated 310 horsepower. With a little more modification, the same V-8 pumped out 355 horsepower through the use of a triple carburetor setup. The message was clear: Cadillac's cars were big, they were long, and, in spite of their size, they were fast.

The absolute king of the fin wars made its debut in 1959. Cadillac introduced the 1959 lineup to a motoring public that thought they had seen it all. An excessive but tasteful use of sheet metal made Cadillac's 1959 lineup everything that a 1950s car

A forlorn 1958 Chevrolet Biscayne looks right at home parked on Main Street U.S.A. Styling for Chevrolet took a left turn for 1958, and a larger and more rounded body saw a reduction of the fin's height. It was now slanted and held two taillights mounted horizontally. Although completely restyled, Chevrolet's 1958 lineup proved immensely popular with the motoring public. Over 1,217,047 Chevrolets were built in the model year.

could be. Its long and sharp tailfin featured two bullet-inspired taillamps that seemed to want to take the car into flight. This quintessential design, which truly demonstrates the ultimate fin of the 1950s, was the design work of noted General Motors design stylist Dave Holls. Holls' double-bullet fin on the 1959 Cadillac has come to represent the entire movement of the fin during the 1950s. If we can credit Harley Earl with starting the fin movement, then we can also credit Holls with taking it to the limit, and also with winding it down in such a way

that it went out with respect. The design of the 1959 Cadillac proved that a tall vertical stabilizer could have a home on a car that couldn't fly. Series 75 Cadillacs rode on a long 149.75-inch wheelbase, while the rest of the lineup used a 130-inch wheelbase. These were not small cars as their extensive use of chrome and breathtaking length were bold designs that spoke of Cadillac's dominance of the fin wars. To be sure, everyone else had their own idea of what the fin should look like, but Cadillac remained in a class all its own.

A new body greeted Chevrolet buyers for 1959, and the fins were once again a prominent part of the new design. A horizontal gull-wing theme and matching cat-eye taillamps made the 1959 lineup a standout in the crowd. This two-door Impala Sport Coupe has been treated to a complete restoration. The Chevrolet Impala and the rest of Chevrolet's lineup proved to be very popular with the public and the GM division built 1,481,071 cars for the model year.

Chrysler had gained a strong foothold in the fin wars by 1956, and with Virgil Exner's "100-million-dollar look" in firm control, the company entered the height of the fin craze with full force. Styling for 1957 was absolutely beautiful as Chrysler took the prestigious *Motor Trend* "Car of the Year" award. Not only were Chrysler's cars illuminating the parking lots of the local country club, but they were also burning up the pavement thanks

to the letter-series cars. Starting in 1955, Chrysler offered the 300 Series cars with power as the main theme. For 1957, Chrysler offered the 300 C convertible, of which only 484 were built. Those that have survived are now commanding premium prices on the collector market. The 300 C had it all: good looks, comfortable interior, and power to spare. The 300 C came with a 392-cubic-inch V-8 that was carbureted with not one, but two four-barrel Carters

Buick was dubbed "The Year's Most Changed Car" when the company introduced an all-new style for 1959. In an attempt to literally change the company's image, old model names were dropped and the new names LeSabre, Invicta, and Electra were now carrying the Buick banner. The bold new style proved to be more than conservative Buick buyers could handle and Buick's sales ranking in the market dropped to a postwar low.

that enabled the big V-8 to crank out an astounding 375 horsepower. Fin design for the 300 C was tall and sweeping across the entire rear length of the car. Chrysler had truly captured the look of the fin without disgracing its original intent. Of premier concern to Chrysler was the comfort of its passengers as the company even offered the optional "Highway HiFi," which allowed the occupants to play their records while traveling the roadways of America.

Luxury as defined by Chrysler in 1958 came in the form of the Imperial. Advertised as "America's most distinctive fine car," the Imperial left no stone unturned when it came to quality and refinement. The Imperial was big with a wheelbase of 129 inches (149.5 for the Crown Imperial) and weighed in at close to 5,000 pounds depending on body style. The Imperial carried a tasteful fin that was set apart from the competition by the use of a circular gun sight–type design that was truly elegant.

Quality control for the Imperial was a major factor in every car built. According to historical records, as many as 17 hours were spent on each car just to ensure that the doors fit perfectly.

When Plymouth introduced its 1958 lineup on October 16, 1957, there was a subtle difference in the fin's height. Plymouth was not apprehensive about maintaining its place in the fin wars. After placing third in American automobile sales in 1957, the company had no intention of relinquishing its place in the market. Crisp, clean, and attractive styling gave the customers just what they wanted. Unfortunately, 1958 would prove to be a recession year for the auto industry with American automobile sales down 22 percent. Despite Plymouth's 34 percent loss in sales, the company still maintained its third-place standing in the market. Plymouth's streamlined styling was clearly evident in the Belvedere two-door hardtop. Riding on a 118-inch wheelbase, the Belvedere featured a 317.6-cubic-inch V-8 that propelled the 3,410-pound car with ease. There was also a subseries on the Belvedere line called the Fury, which came only in a two-door sport coupe and featured a tweaked engine that managed a respectable 290 horsepower. A wonderful array of two-tone body colors

Virgil Exner's work for Chrysler during the 1950s took the company's design work to higher standards. Chrysler caught onto the fin idea relatively early in the game, and by 1957, it had fins that were riding with the best. The powerful 1957 300C was a car of stunning beauty, and it was a lively performer. Detroit was just beginning to cultivate the musclecar phenomenon that would reach its height in the 1960s.

Pontiac introduced the beautiful Bonneville for 1957. Availability was limited to one per dealer for the stylish Bonneville, which contained a number of design features that indicated Pontiac's direction for the coming years. Fuel injection was featured on the Bonneville, of which only 630 were built for the year. There was no shortage of bright work on Pontiac's wonderful creation, which helped sell the rest of the line. Pontiac would be the nation's sixth-largest automobile builder in 1957.

enhanced Plymouth's appeal. There was certainly no doubt that Plymouth was in the thick of the fin wars, and would go to great lengths to keep up with the competition.

Another Chrysler division, DeSoto, made good use of its sheet metal by building the Adventurer. The Adventurer was DeSoto's top-of-the-line offering for 1959, and it was in a class all by itself. A triple-taillight fin set it apart from everything else on the road. The Adventurer, a car of stunning elegance, was also a lively performer thanks to its 383-cubic-inch V-8 that used two four-barrel

carburetors. DeSoto would build only 97 Adventurer convertibles for 1959, making it a very rare car in today's collector market. Extensive use of gold anodized trim on the rear quarter panels gave a look of true elegance.

While Ford's stylists were building some of the most far-out designs ever seen in the styling studios, production Fords continued the tradition of restrained elegance for the late 1950s. For 1957, the Thunderbird received a face-lift that lengthened the rear of the car. Fins now played a prominent part on the Thunderbird, although they were

In a design that could only have come from the aviation industry, the 1957 Bonneville made no attempt to hide its jet-styled inspiration. The entire assembly mimicked the jet age in every way. Pontiac proved that the height of the fin didn't necessarily have to be tall in order to garner attention. The extensive use of chrome and stainless steel said it all.

The Pontiac Safari wagon was a classy way to haul the American family around. Plenty of upper-line trim appointments made the Safari a wonderful way to hit the open road for the family vacation. This 1957 Star Chief Custom Safari two-door wagon has already achieved Milestone status.

still relatively small when compared to the competition. Nevertheless, the fin treatment on Ford's 1957 Thunderbird proved to be a wonderful design, as the company would build 21,380 Thunderbirds for the motoring public. Ford's 1957 Thunderbird would turn out to be the last of the two-seaters. Nineteen fifty-eight saw the Thunderbird grow into a four-seater that changed the personality of the Thunderbird forever.

Full-size Fords also benefited from the designers' use of restrained elegance, as Ford would out-produce rival Chevrolet to become America's number one automobile producer for the 1957 model year. The big news for 1957 was the addition of the Skyliner. The Skyliner was a convertible hard-top that featured a completely disappearing roof. What amazed the public even more was that all of this happened with the touch of a button. Because

For 1958, Pontiac's Bonneville received a new body that was as smooth and graceful as any car of the fin era. Power was still a major theme with Pontiac, as the Bonneville would use a 370-cubic-inch engine that generated 285 horsepower. Two-tone color treatments made for an attractive package in the Bonneville lineup.

the mechanism was a complex series of servos and relays, it was truly an impressive sight. The retractable roof was interesting to say the least, but a restoration of one of Ford's complex Skyliners is a challenge that most would shy away from.

By the height of the fin wars in 1959, Ford's lineup again proved that less was better. As the American public gobbled up anything with wings on the rear quarters, Ford chose a classic design that earned the company a Gold Medal for Exceptional Styling at the Brussels World Fair. Ford's stark defiance of the superfin craze of 1959 was a brave undertaking. In the face of the competition, Ford proved that good taste could still be found in the simplistic design of an automobile. In 1960, Ford would redesign its fin and it would become a mere horizontal slant on the rear deck. To credit Ford's design studios, Ford certainly had the resources and the design inspiration to build fins with the rest of Detroit, but for the most part the company chose to remain on the sidelines of the fin wars.

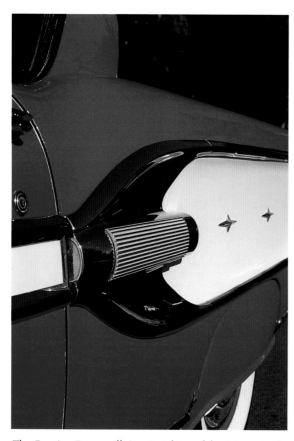

The Pontiac Bonneville's mimicking of the jet age took matters one step further for 1958 and used a jetlike air intake on its rear quarter just aft of the door. The half-cylinder set off by an upper and lower trim sweep was an inspirational trim piece that spoke directly to the aviation theme of the day.

If Ford was showing restraint in its use of the fin, rival Chevrolet was more than making up for it in their 1957 lineup. Chevrolet grafted a huge fin onto the 1957s that would go on to become an icon of the classic fin era. Changes for Chevrolet were clearly evident as a new front bumper made its debut. Chevrolet made good use of a gold anodized finish on the grille work up front, and redesigned headlight assemblies containing air

intakes for the interior made for a beautiful, yet functional, front end. The hood featured two menacing rocket-inspired pods that directly reflected the aeronautic theme of the day. Chevrolet would offer three series for 1957 with body trim appointments signifying the difference between the One-Fifty, Two-Ten, and the Bel Air. No matter what the buyer was able to afford, all models came with those wonderful fins. In a neat styling trick that fooled many gas-station attendants, Chevrolet hid the fuel filler cap behind the chrome housing on the rear of the left fin. Chevrolet's beautiful design for 1957 was a hit on any model, but perhaps is best displayed on the Bel Air convertible. In what would be a very close race, Chevrolet would build only 144 more cars than Ford in 1957, but Ford would beat Chevrolet in model year production, thus making Ford the nation's number one automobile builder. Once again, Ford's restrained design proved popular with the motoring public.

For 1958, Chevrolet would take a side road in terms of its fin development and actually tone down the fin's height and sharpness. Gone was the sharklike dorsal fin that sat so predominately on the 1957s, and in its place was a rounded fin that featured two taillights set horizontally apart from one another. While most of Detroit was operating on the two-year plan—where a new body style was introduced every two years with a face-lift in between—Chevrolet had been face-lifting its lineup for the past three years. The 1958 models represented the last of Harley Earl's reign at GM, and Bill Mitchell would now lead GM's styling. The 1958s would prove to be a one-year wonder, as 1959 would see the introduction of a universal body that brought GM, and the fin, back in line. Chevrolet's lineup for 1959 featured a sleek new body that was definitely at home in the late 1950s. A new tailfin design that resembled a gull-wing

Rambler's Ambassador was well appointed for 1958 and featured a sharp fin on the rear. Rambler would be the only car company to increase sales in the recession year of 1958. The Ambassador was a lively performer, thanks to its 327-cubic-inch V-8 rated at 270 horsepower. Rambler would cross over into the 1960s with the guidance of company president George Romney, and would prove to be very successful in the coming years.

affair was very attractive on the low-slung body. Chevrolet's fin for 1959 was literally laid over horizontally in a design that was different from any fin yet seen. Clearly, the era of the large rounded lines inspired by Harley Earl had passed.

Another GM division, Buick, was also all new for 1959. In an attempt to change its image, Buick even changed the names of its models for 1959. Gone was the low-end Special, replaced by the name LeSabre. The midlevel Buick previously known as the Century now carried the name Invicta, and the top-of-the-line model was now known as the Electra and Electra 225, replacing the Super and the Roadmaster. Everything about the new Buick was a radical departure from Buick's traditional sense of styling. The new Buick was longer, lower, and wider. Headlights were set at an angle, as were the fins on the rear. Simple bullet-nosed taillights sat below the huge fins. Buick advertised that these cars didn't even look like Buicks, and the

Even radio antennas were not safe from the aviation-inspired designs of the day. Rambler's Ambassador featured an antenna that was mounted in the middle of the trunk and was swept back to imitate the dorsal fin of one of the many jets of the era. Plenty of chrome set the Ambassador apart from the rest of Rambler's offerings for 1958.

general public agreed. The new style proved to be more than traditional Buick buyers could handle and sales dropped to a postwar low. Although they were not a hit with the public when introduced, the 1959 Buicks with their huge diagonal tailfins are a true representation of the late-1950s fin.

Not to be left out in the cold, Pontiac was sporting some of the most beautiful cars ever to roll out of Detroit during the late 1950s. In 1957, Pontiac aimed its marketing plans directly at the younger generation. The infamous Silver Streak styling theme that had been a mainstay at Pontiac for so many years was removed. In a move that set Pontiac apart from all of the rest, Pontiac's fin would not be the big feature in the car's design, but rather its adornment of trim work would be its claim to fame, even though Pontiac's fin would be absolutely jetlike in its appearance. It is rumored that one owner of a 1957 Pontiac noted that children would not stand near the rear of the car for fear of being burned by the jet blast. Side spear treatments and a multitude of color schemes set Pontiac apart from the competition. All new for 1957 was the limited-run Bonneville, which came only in a fuel-injected convertible. At $5,782, the Bonneville was the most expensive Pontiac by far and only 630 Bonnevilles were built for 1957, which makes them very rare in today's collector market.

Another offering from Pontiac was the Safari wagon. Luxurious appointments again set the Safari apart from the competition. As a two-door wagon, the Safari introduced the American family to a sporty way to take the all-important summer vacation. Safaris were powered by Pontiac's 347-cubic-inch V-8, making them lively performers as well. If there was any doubt that the trim-laden Pontiacs were inspired by the aviation industry, they were quickly put to rest when the 1958 Pontiac Bonneville hit the streets. In a move that must have been borrowed from Lockheed's Starfighter jet, the 1958 Bonneville featured a jetlike air intake pod that sat just aft of the doors. Fins were redesigned for 1958, and they now sat horizontally with two taillights housed in the rear pod. Overall, the late 1950s would see wonderful cars from the Pontiac division.

Packard and Studebaker had also jumped in with both feet as fins were an intricate part of each car's design. One of the last of the independents, Rambler was still fighting for survival in the thick of the fin wars, but made great strides during the late 1950s. After a merger that saw the marriage of Nash-Kelvinator, and Hudson became known as American Motors Corporation, the company made the decision to drop the Nash and Hudson names for 1958. Instead they would concentrate on selling a revised series of cars and a newer version of the original Rambler compact car. While the Rambler American was completely devoid of the fin, it did offer economy at a good price, which was something that the American public warmed up to in the recession year of 1958. Those who wanted Rambler's quality with a set of fins could choose

from any of Rambler's other offerings. The company would boast a sales increase in the recession year of 1958 and would be the only automobile company to do so as all others declined in sales. Rambler had the good fortune of having the right car at the right time.

The years 1957 through 1959 proved to be the very pinnacle of fin design for the American automobile. Longer and lower bodies mated to large-horsepower engines were the order of the day. Never before and never again would the motoring public have the chance to buy such wonderful cars. As America crossed over into the 1960s, the fin would begin to diminish and the nation would forever leave the decade of innocence. Yes, it was almost over, but some of Detroit's car builders still had a few tricks up their sleeves.

Cadillac's new design for 1959 would prove to be the absolute pinnacle for fin design of the 1950s. Longer and lower bodies accented by an extreme fin that housed twin bullet-like taillights was an attractive style that the public loved. The 1959 Cadillacs had a wheelbase of 149.75 inches on the Series 75, and 130 inches on the remaining models. The flowing lines of the two-door hardtop made the Coupe DeVille look even longer than it actually was. This example is finshed in Kensington Green.

5

Winding Down

By 1960, the fin had begun to play itself out. As with any fad, the general public's interest in the fin began to wane. America was now entering the decade of the 1960s, and the age of innocence was beginning to slip away. Although Americans did not yet realize it, they were about to enter a decade of turmoil. Over the course of the next several years the nation would be shattered by a missile crisis, the assassination of an American president, and U.S. entrance into a war from which there

After several years of contention in the fin wars, Mercury chose a look of simplicity for its top-of-the-line 1960 Park Lane. The rear bumper housed a dramatic taillight lens that featured extreme vertical height and was accented by a tastefully curved fin. Mercury chose to keep the fin alive for a few more years despite the fact that most others were eliminating it by the early 1960s. A small fin could be seen on Mercury's lineup into the 1963 model year.

Cadillac introduced a simplified and more elegant automobile for 1960. The company that had literally invented the chrome-accented wonders of the 1950s was now shedding the "more is better" theme in favor of sheer beauty. The twin bullet lights of 1959 were replaced by a streamlined lens that was mounted on the trailing edge of its bladed fin. The Eldorado Seville two-door hardtop was especially elegant in Cadillac's hue of Champagne with an Olympic White Vicodec fabric roof.

would be no easy return. The decade of the 1950s was gone, but the fin would remain a factor in several of Detroit's designs.

After the design-shattering statement made by the fin, it was almost impossible to just eliminate it overnight. Instead, most car manufacturers chose to decrease the fin's visual impact a little each year until it was completely eliminated on most cars by the mid-1960s. Many car manufacturers crossed into the decade with a new design causing vast changes to the fin. Conservative styling began to reign supreme, and many marques drastically reduced the amount of chrome on their new offerings as well. Although the fin would soldier on for a few more years, gone were the days when bigger was better. American Motors had proven that there was room in the market for a finless economy car in 1958 with the Rambler American, and more Americans began to recognize the cost-saving measures of a smaller car. The dinosaur-sized cruiser of the

For 1961, Cadillac offered some major styling changes that had been previewed on the 1959 and 1960 Eldorado Broughams. The bodies were wonderfully sculptured with sweeping horizontal lines that featured a full-length lower-body skeg that matched the upper fin at the rear quarter. The lower skeg fin had been previewed on the 1959 Cyclone show car. A minor recession in 1961 resulted in a total production run of 138,379 cars against 1960's total of 142,184. The most visual change in the rear was the taillight treatment, which now ran horizontally just above the bumper. This 1961 Coupe DeVille is finished in Laredo Tan.

1950s was on its way to extinction, but it wouldn't die with a bang. Instead it would slowly creep out of style just as gracefully as it had crept in.

Luxury car leader Cadillac made extensive changes for 1960. Gone was the double bullet taillights mounted on the fin and in was a new sharply bladed appendage. The look that had ruled 1959 was now a victim of the past. Cadillac's fin was now a sleek and streamlined design that took Cadillac to new highs in terms of elegant simplicity. A new full-width grille coupled with a noticeable reduction in the amount of trim made for a more conservative styling statement. The new Cadillacs were more elegant in their "less is more" theme for 1960, but Cadillac's fin would begin its steady decline from this point forward.

A restyled Cadillac greeted buyers in 1961. Cadillac continued to tone down its offerings by making a concession to the economy market, something that the general public wasn't ready to accept in the nation's premier luxury car. A new Short Deck Sedan was introduced in the Series 62 lineup. The new Short Deck Sedan was a full 7 inches shorter than other production-model Cadillacs.

Chevrolet's 1960 Impala continued the use of a gull-wing–type fin that made for an attractive and classic look. A linear design that saw an upper trim line extend all the way back to the rear fin was aerodynamic and slippery. An aircraft-inspired side trim treatment proved that space exploration and aviation were still major factors in American automobile design. Chevrolet's fin for 1960 is displayed nicely on this Impala convertible finished in Roman Red.

Buyers rejected the shortened Series 62 and in the end only 3,756 were built. Competition for Cadillac's 1961 lineup included an all-new design of the Lincoln Continental that included a four-door convertible. The Lincoln's design was stunning, and despite the fact that fins were not a prominent feature, it is recognized today as one of the most outstanding automobiles to ever grace the roadways.

Chevrolet introduced a face-lift on its 1960 lineup and made only slight changes to its models. The graceful swanlike fins from 1959 now had a more angular look and the cat's-eye rear taillights were replaced by a more traditional lens that was set in a beauty panel. The gorgeous wraparound windshield continued for 1960, and styling was especially classy on the two-door hardtop and convertible. Chevrolet's lineup for 1961 saw its fin reduced to a mere ridge line running across the rear quarter and rounding the rear deck, and a restyle in 1962 saw the fin disappear from Chevrolet's models forever. The company that had produced the classically finned Bel Air from 1957 was now marching headlong into the musclecar era with its Super Sport and Corvette models. The

After a dismal sales year in 1959, Buick chose to face-lift its body in hopes of winning back traditional Buick buyers. A new look for 1960 was achieved by rounding the bodylines and sculpturing the sides for an effect that was pleasing from any angle. In an attempt to bring traditional Buick buyers back into the showrooms, ventiports were reintroduced for 1960. Buick still retained its new model names with the LeSabre, Invicta, Electra, and Electra 225 carrying the Buick banner for 1960.

company's focus had changed, and the fin was no longer a design factor in Chevrolet's lineup.

The writing was also on the wall at Buick where lessons learned from the previous year were hard at work. Buick continued to share many components with several of its GM counterparts, but the 1960 design was more than just a face-lift. In order to increase sales, Buick knew that it could not rely on the previous year's design, which proved to be disastrous in terms of the public's acceptance. Buick's fin was thus toned down, clipped, and rounded while the sides and front received a little more artwork in the form of sculptured bodylines. Ventiports returned in 1960, most likely in an ill-fated attempt to lure back some of the more traditional Buick buyers. In the end the

Buick's fin was toned down for 1960, and a more rounded look now reigned. The angle of Buick's fin was still sharp, and it still carried a look of elegance from the rear. The conservative refinements would not help, as Buick would slip even further down the industry sales ladder. Nevertheless, Buick's Invicta was a well-balanced design that remains a big hit at the local car shows today.

Pontiac drastically altered its fin for 1960 by reducing its visual height and trim work. After years of excessive amounts of chrome and body styles that spoke directly to the aviation movement of the 1950s, Pontiac would cross into the 1960s with a look that gave a strong indication of GM's direction in the near future. Pontiac was quickly shedding its stodgy postwar image and focusing on performance. In a few short years the musclecar movement would begin to awaken, giving birth to such legendary cars as the GTO and Firebird.

face-lift didn't work, as Buick would sell fewer cars in 1960 than during its postwar low in 1959. In fact, Buick would produce 253,999 cars for the model year in 1960, earning it a ninth-place ranking in industry sales. This was Buick's lowest ranking in the industry since 1905. Although they were not a big hit when new, the modern collector market has recognized the 1959 and 1960 Buicks as one of the premier cruisers of the fin era. Buick would spend the decade of the 1960s redefining itself as a

performance car builder and would go on to produce the Wildcat and the Riviera in an attempt to entice younger buyers. The fin would quietly leave Buick in 1961.

The year 1960 would mark another restyle for Pontiac. The only body component that did not change was the roof. A new hood, grille, and sculptured fender all came together at a point to form a front end that was sharp and attractive. On the rear, Pontiac would be one of Detroit's first to

Plymouth chose to carry its extreme vertical fin into 1960 as the Savoy clearly demonstrates. The extremely tall appendage was in stark contrast to the competition, which was now reducing the overall height of the fin. Plymouth did have the foresight to carry the Valiant as a concession to the growing economy market. Plymouth would also restyle in 1961, and its fin would pass into history, as a flat deck would grace the rear of all full-size Plymouths.

completely abandon the vertical appeal of the tail-fin. Instead, the rear taillights were held in two rather simplistic pods that made no attempt to be the focal point of the car. Overall, Pontiac chose the theme of simplicity, form, and function for 1960. Pontiac would spend the 1960s concentrating on the musclecar as the wonderful Grand Prix, GTO, and Firebird would go on to burn up the streets of America. Pontiac had entered a new age, and the book was now closed on Pontiac's era of the fin.

One of the few car manufacturers that continued to offer a large fin into the 1960 model year was Plymouth. While others were toning down

their use of the fin, Plymouth's huge dorsal fin continued to resemble the jets that inspired it. Plymouth had an eye on the future when it marketed the Valiant line for Chrysler in 1960 as a concession to the growing movement toward economy. The Valiant proved to be very successful due to its economical price. The rest of the Plymouth line received a rework of its front-end sheet metal that used an unusual side cove treatment just ahead of the front wheels. While this would be Plymouth's last year of the fin, it wouldn't just drift out as others had done. Plymouth would literally cross from 1960 to 1961 by completely eliminating the fin. In a demonstration of Plymouth's extended use of the

The 1961 model year would be the last of Virgil Exner's fin design at Chrysler. Chrysler's fin had now gained a look of elegance, and its trailing edge was a sharply angled affair that fit nicely on the finely sculptured lines of its cars. The fins adorning this Newport Town & Country wagon finished in Sahara Tan add a look of refinement that was the crowning end of Exner's contribution to the fin wars.

now-waning fin, Rambler would move into third place for 1960, pushing Plymouth into forth.

As with everyone else, Chrysler also toned down the fin as it crossed into the new decade. For 1960, Chrysler featured a restyled body with a fin that was slightly altered for the new model. The tailfin design was lengthened for 1961, and this would be the last year that Virgil Exner gave input into the fin's design. The man who had led Chrysler through the era of finned elegance was now entering the latter part of his exciting career. Exner would remain a Chrysler consultant until 1964, and he remained active by starting his own private industrial design firm with his son. Exner passed away on December 22, 1973, and with his passing came the end of an era in automotive design history.

While most car builders were scrambling for new designs that signaled the end of the fin, Ford would have no trouble reducing the height of its fin due to the fact that its fin had never reached astronomical proportions. In particular, Mercury usually employed tasteful styling tactics, and their graceful exit from the 1950s would showcase a linear design that crossed into the new decade of the 1960s with a classic look. After experimenting with several different versions of the fin in the late 1950s, Mercury decided that it had enough. A straight and simple line, beginning at the rear door edge and extending back to its large oval taillight,

By 1962, Mercury had erased most of the fins on the Monterey although there was still a slight rise on the rear quarter panel. The small fin ended with a circular pod that housed the taillight. The overall appearance of the Monterey clearly demonstrated the direction of Mercury for the decade of the 1960s. Strangely enough, Mercury would resurrect a fin for 1963 on the Monterey, and its Comet and Meteor line still carried a small fin until 1963.

DeSoto's last stand came in 1961, as the once proud marque would cease production in November of 1960. This beautiful 1961 DeSoto is finished in Mediterranean Blue and has a mere 35,000 miles on the odometer. DeSoto still represented good value for the money in 1961, and power came from a 361-cubic-inch V-8 that featured 265 horsepower. Note the extreme lateral length of DeSoto's last fin; it begins at the front door and extends all the way back to the rear deck.

had its formerly proud fin slumping over in a curved fashion. The look was fresh and didn't detract from the overall appearance of Mercury's cars for 1960. For 1962, Mercury's fin was still prevalent in its Comet model, but the Monterey's fin treatment was merely a small lateral hump that housed a single taillamp at the rear. To be fair, Mercury kept a small hint of the fin alive for several years after the bubble burst, but it would never again see the vertical height of the late 1950s.

A sad note would mar the beginning of the decade as the once proud DeSoto would pass into history. After years of providing solid transportation to the American motoring public, DeSoto would cease to exist on November 30, 1960. The recession year of 1958 was not kind to DeSoto, which saw a 60 percent decline in production. DeSoto limped through its last few years as many had already predicted the demise of the marque. The last DeSotos produced would bear close resemblance to their Chrysler counterparts, with a slightly reworked fin for its last year. There were many who mourned the passing of the DeSoto, but its memory is kept alive today by numerous enthusiasts who gain gratification from owning a car that's a little unusual. DeSoto's contribution to the

The angled look of DeSoto's fin for 1961 was in stark contrast to the tall vertical standing fin of 1959. In a clear demonstration of the fin's refinement over the years, it had grown up and out, but had finally come to rest at an angle. The fin had truly made its mark in the course of American car design. Note the absence of excessive chrome and linear influence on the surrounding brightwork.

fin wars of the late 1950s certainly should not be underestimated. Fins were a dominant design feature for DeSoto during the height of the fin craze, and its triple taillight theme still reigns supreme as a hallmark in the entire fin movement.

The 1960s would also claim another great automobile, as Studebaker would not see the end of the decade. After turning out cars for generations of Americans, Studebaker's luck in the crowded 1960s market wouldn't last long. Studebaker fared well in the immediate postwar market when automobile-starved Americans bought anything on

wheels, but as the tide changed in favor of the buyers in the early 1950s, Studebaker began to feel the pressure of a crowded car market. A merger with Packard in 1954 was not enough to stem the flow of red ink, but Studebaker would survive through the 1950s and would produce some stylish cars. Studebaker was also a prominent player in the fin wars with cars such as the Hawk. Studebaker took a cue from Rambler and introduced the economy-minded Lark in 1959. The Lark would help the company through the lean times. Studebaker tried hard to survive in the car market, but in the end the company was outgunned by the big players in the automobile industry. The company that had started by making horse-drawn wagons in 1852 closed its doors in 1966.

The last traditional fin for the American car can be credited to Cadillac. As the company that began the entire movement back in 1948, it was only fitting that it would lead the fin movement out. Cadillac's design for 1964 featured a small fin that was a mere shadow of its former self. The once proud vertical stabilizer that been a hallmark of Cadillac's design for so many years was now just a sharply contoured appendage to the rear quarter that still managed to project a proud connection to its past. By now the general public had grown weary of the fin and it no longer had a place as a prominent feature in American car design. The next year, 1965, would see the end of the once glorious fin, as the new models featured all-new finless styling. Cadillac's rear quarter design would feature sharp vertical lines for several more years, but the traditional vertical fin was now gone. A chapter in Cadillac's history that had literally defined its dominance of the luxury car market had come to a close.

The tailfin left as quietly as it had entered the American automobile scene. While they are

Famed designer Brooks Stevens was contracted to rework Studebaker's Hawk for 1962. Stevens' illustrious career featured several milestones including the Willys Overland Jeepster and the Luxury Liner bicycle. There were only minor changes to the 1963 Hawk's exterior, and the look was typical of the immediate post–fin era as the fin's influence was drastically reduced. This 1963 Gran Turismo Hawk is finished in Rose Mist and features Studebaker's R2 Supercharged V-8. Studebaker was operating on life support and losing ground to the major carmakers by the early 1960s. Still, the company would produce some fine automobiles until production ceased in 1966.

Signaling the end of the fin era, the 1964 Cadillac was the last to carry Harley Earl's original creation. To be fair there would be a bladed peak on Cadillac's long and straight fenders for several more years, but the traditional fin was now a part of automotive history. What had started with a simple hump on the 1948 Series 62 had grown to unheard-of proportions, and then had quietly withdrawn from the American automobile. This 1964 Fleetwood is finished in Cadillac's pleasant hue of Beacon Blue.

certainly gone, they are not forgotten. A walk around any given car show is bound to turn up a few of the fin warriors from days gone by. Was it just a design concession to the aviation industry, or did it really capture the hearts and minds of a generation? We in the modern millennium are left to ponder this fascinating design aspect of automotive history. There wasn't anything like it previously, and there will never be anything like it again. It was a time when the likes of James Dean and Marilyn Monroe ruled the drive-in movie screen. It was a time when Elvis and Chuck Berry ruled the airwaves. But most of all, it was a time of some the most fascinating cars that ever rolled out of Detroit. Fins remain an important hallmark in the history of the American automobile. The finned era of the automobile exists not only in the cars that it created, but it lives on in the hearts and minds of a generation of Americans.

INDEX

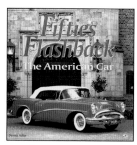

**Fifties Flashback:
The American Car**
ISBN: 0-7603-0126-3

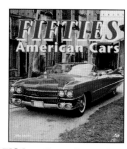

Fifties American Cars
ISBN: 0-87938-924-9

The American Car Dealership
ISBN: 0-7603-0639-7

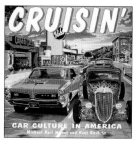

Cruisin': Car Culture in America
ISBN: 0-7603-0148-4

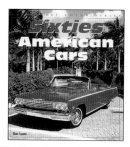

Sixties American Cars
ISBN: 0-7603-0327-4

Chevrolet's Hot Ones
ISBN: 0-7603-0759-8

Chevrolets of the 50's
ISBN: 0-87938-816-1

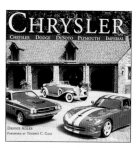

Chrysler
ISBN: 0-7603-0695-8

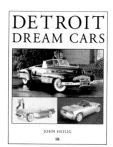

Detroit Dream Cars
ISBN: 0-7603-0838-1